MONMOUTHSHIRE

by

OLIVE PHILLIPS

Illustrated and with a Map

London
Robert Hale Limited
18 Bedford Square WC1

First published 1951

315

PRINTED AND BOUND IN GREAT BRITAIN BY
WILLIAM CLOWES AND SONS LTD, LONDON AND BECCLES

The County Books Series
GENERAL EDITOR: BRIAN VESEY-FITZGERALD

MONMOUTHSHIRE

THE COUNTY BOOKS SERIES

A series comprising 57 volumes. It covers every county in England and there will be five books on Scotland, two on Ireland, two on the Hebrides, and one each on Orkney, Shetland, Wales, the Isle of Man and the Channel Islands

THE FOLLOWING FORTY-ONE VOLUMES
HAVE NOW BEEN PUBLISHED

PLEASE WRITE TO THE PUBLISHERS
FOR FULL DESCRIPTIVE PROSPECTUS

To mother
in memory of my father
who loved Monmouthshire

CONTENTS

ILLUSTRATIONS

ix

ILLUSTRATIONS

Present-day difficulties do not permit of a comprehensive map of the area being included in this book. For more detailed information, readers are referred to the respective Ordnance Survey sheets.

ACKNOWLEDGMENT

All of the above illustrations are reproduced from photographs supplied by Mr W. T. Barber of Newport.

x

INTRODUCTION

I SUPPOSE one day someone is going to make Monmouthshire officially Welsh in all respects so that we do not have to be referred to as "South Wales and Monmouthshire", and people with a definite trace of Welsh accent in their speech will have a harder job to assert their belief that they are English. I would not like to say what we are, because the controversy always becomes so fierce.

"Lovely day, aye", says the Valley man, and he sounds as Welsh as his Taff Valley neighbour. Perhaps towards Chepstow the Gloucestershire burr can be heard in the speech, but the lilt of Wales is never far away; while on the Herefordshire border the broader tone is obvious.

Monmouthshire has been a county since 1536. Gwent, still used as the local name of Monmouthshire, was a cantref (or portion) of Morganwg, and Wentllwg (more commonly known today as Wentlloog) was another, until in 1536 the new county of Monmouth was set up by Henry VIII. This was done by separating Gwent and Wentllwg from Morganwg. Morganwg spread from the River Tawe to the Wye, with the northern limits much as they are today. Wentllwg was the cantref between the Rhymney and the Usk rivers, while Gwent formed the fertile land between Usk and Wye. Today, Wentllwg is the name of the coastal strip between Rhymney and Usk, while Gwent covers the whole of Monmouthshire. Gwent itself was divided into Gwent Uchcoed and Gwent Iscoed —above the wood and below the wood—the areas each side of the once great forest of Wentwood.

Probably the earliest settlers in Wales were the

I

Iberians, a Mediterranean race, dark and small, whose descendants are found in the central districts of old "Morganwg", the present-day industrial valleys of Glamorgan and Monmouthshire. The later Celtic races who stayed in Wales were sometimes tall, and often with red hair. Two of the Celtic races, the Brythons and the Goidels, made most impression as far as a way of living was concerned. It is a form of the Brythonic language which is "Welsh" as we know it today. Various settlers came from time to time, and the races intermingled, but it seems that the purest of the old races, in South Wales at any rate, are probably the Iberian types in their mountain strongholds. They were a difficult people to draw from the fastness of the hills, and even today they retain an individual outlook and a racial resemblance to their forebears.

When the Romans invaded Britain, the Silures, who were the tribe inhabiting the south-east of Wales, and who were presumably a mixture of the races which had settled in the district, refused to be conquered. They were living mainly in hill-forts, and had the protection of natural land barriers. Continually they harassed the Roman armies, retiring to the hills until the next attack. Although they were fierce fighters, and in many ways primitive compared with the Romans, they were by no means uncivilised. Under the leadership of Caractacus they foiled the invader many times, and after the capture of their leader still they held out, causing trouble while the rest of the land was at peace. Their eventual defeat came about A.D. 78, some thirty years after the beginning of the Roman invasion of Britain.

One early eighteenth-century historian gives this account:

"But the Silures, the bravest and most powerful of all the Britons, could not be tam'd, either by Clemency or severity. Their Forces were so considerable that the Legions were obliged to march against them. They were headed by their King Caractacus, famous for his great Exploits, and universally esteemed by his Countrymen, being accounted the best General Britain had ever produced. This Prince, whom the Nations in alliance with the Silures had made Commander in Chief, was retired into the Country of the Ordovices (inhabitants of Montgomeryshire, Merionethshire, Caernarvonshire, Flintshire, Denbighshire), where assembling all his Forces, he resolves to expect the Romans."

Caerleon, the military fortress where the Second Augusta Legion, under Julius Frontinus, was stationed, seemed to have no immediate reaction upon the rebellious Silures when it was built about A.D. 74 or 75. The Romans then tried gentle persuasion, and soon after Caerleon fortress was begun, a new civil town was founded at Caerwent, a model of luxurious living, with a comfort that the Silures in their hill-forts could not have known. This brought the Silures down from their strongholds to test the new-found way of living, and by A.D. 78 there was no more trouble from them.

The fall of Rome came gradually, and by the fifth century was almost complete, and for all the luxury that the Romans had brought, they left no great impression on the local people. A certain intermingling of races there must have been, and some characteristics of the Romans must have remained, but the towns fell into decay, and the life of the natives went on without great change. From then on the Welsh suffered the same waves of invasions

3

that the rest of Britain endured: from the Saxons, and also the Danes, who were once badly defeated by the Silures at Tidenham, near Chepstow, after dreadful ravages. In 896 the Danes made their greatest attack on Mercia and several Welsh districts, including Gwent, which laid much of the land to waste. From 918 to 952 there was a comparatively peaceful period: but the Welsh soon found unrest among themselves, and this was always a hindrance in the numerous border risings of the Norman heyday.

Never was there such a time of treachery on all sides as when the Marcher lordships were created in the eleventh and twelfth centuries. The Welsh could never really be conquered, but there would have been more progress against the barons had there been more unity. Perhaps two of the leaders who did most in this direction were Llywelyn ap Iorwerth, known as Llywelyn the Great, and Llywelyn ap Gruffydd, his grandson. The two Llywelyns, in their own periods, were responsible for bringing together all the Welsh princes as a fairly united body, and Llywelyn ap Gruffydd became the last native Prince of Wales, in 1248, having achieved almost complete unity within Wales. (The use of surnames was unknown at this time, "ap" signifying "son of", and going on indefinitely, generation after generation, as when Llywelyn ap Gruffydd's father is writen down as Gruffydd ap Llywelyn ap Iorwerth).

All along the Welsh border the Normans built their castles, which were to change hands many times over the years. The circumstances led to corruption among the Normans and rebellion from the Welsh, and the border lands must have been troubled beyond comprehension. The barons were often cruel, but to estimate their actions

4

it is necessary to think that men's standards in certain respects have altered very considerably—and not only were the Normans cruel: the Welsh, too, matched the mood. Later, in chapters when castles are brought to life in their own periods, the old stories can be told. This is merely an over-all, and brief, introduction to the main changes in early Welsh history, in which Gwent played its part as a true border district.

Not only were the Normans attempting to subdue the Welsh, but they were also using the troubles for their own gain, sometimes fighting between themselves, and by 1284 Edward I had annexed Wales to the English Crown. This was not done entirely to have the Welsh under his rule, but to keep his Norman barons in a little more order, as they were becoming too strong for safety. Under the new arrangement, the barons were responsible to the King. The Edwardian conquest came after the death in battle of Llywelyn ap Gruffydd, whose severed head was sent to Edward, for the great leader had gone and the unity was broken.

The greatest battles were fought after Edward's Statute of Wales, and rose to a climax in the early fifteenth century when Owain Glyndwr rose against the barons, bringing with him the loyalty of Welshmen and a certain mysticism that upset the English soldiers before they went into battle. So little is known with any certainty of Glyndwr that Shakespeare's description in *Henry IV* is rather apt to be taken as historically true. It is Glyndwr's own description, too, led on by Hotspur's mocking. After telling of fiery shapes and the earth trembling at the time of his birth, he goes on, ". . . I am not in the roll of common men". This must have been true enough. No common man, indeed. He was able to lead his people, in some sort of unity, to prevent the complete conquest of Wales. Yet on the English and Welsh sides there was treachery, and savage acts of revenge were carried out, marking this as a period of sorrow in Welsh history. In its turn, Gwent suffered in the reign of bloodshed when Owain Glyndwr made his locust-like travels through the Marcher lands. Castles and churches, secular or sacred, all were treated with similar disregard; yet behind the leader of fighting men was Glyndwr the patriot, who wanted to see Wales independent, with its own parliament, church, and university.

Although in theory the annexing of Wales to the English Crown should have curbed the power of the Marcher barons, in execution they still carried on in the old way, becoming more troublesome than the native Welsh, who were comparatively peaceful when left to themselves, and showed great loyalty during the French wars. When Henry VIII came to the throne, the time was ready for the prevention of the dissatisfaction, warlike conditions, and the threat of the Marcher lords. A new system of ruling came into force, breaking up the old lordships by making them a definite part of England and not merely a portion of the annexed Principality. The two cantrefs already mentioned, Gwent and Wentllwg, were, then, separated from Wales officially, yet their natural characteristics, both racial and geographical, were not English, and have never become entirely English. This applies particularly to the western area.

That part of the land which became Monmouthshire is still not sure where it is. Officially English, by order of Henry VIII, its sons are capped by Wales in the world of sport, it is looked after physically by the Welsh Board of Health, is educated by the Welsh Board of Education

—and its licensing laws are obviously those of Wales, but Henry VIII had nothing to do with that.

Because this book is about Monmouthshire, then my plan must be the same as the natural plan of the county. Monmouthshire is divided by its river valleys cutting through the hills. It is not easy to be precise in such a segregation, as district merges into district, and perhaps the tributary of a rural river runs into an industrial area. Then again, there are other outstanding features which do not come into the river valleys and need a chapter to themselves. But to see a relief map of the county is to see that the land is cut from north to south by a succession of rivers.

There is the Rhymney which forms the boundary on the Glamorgan side; the Sirhowy and the Ebbw, both with industry along their banks, and the tributaries of these rivers. Although industry lies thick in these valleys, one is never far from the country in Gwent; of different nature, true, but it is there all the same.

After the stark beauty and dark towns of the mountains and steep valleys, and the atmosphere of heavy industries, there are the Soar, the Candwr, and the Olway, tributaries —often little more than brooks—of the Usk, which, with the main river, wind through some lovely country.

The Wye Valley is the one part of Monmouthshire— and it is shared with other counties—that is widely known.

From Christchurch, on the outskirts of Newport, the wooded ridge known as Wentwood runs parallel with the River Usk for some miles, then continues almost to Chepstow, in view of the main Newport to Chepstow road. The Royal Chase of Wentwood once spread over a much larger area than that which we call Wentwood today, and some of the protective fortresses still remain.

The villages of Grosmont and Skenfrith, with their

7

castles, which make the triangle of fortresses with White
Castle, form part of northern Monmouthshire, set in
absolutely grand country, and together with the Vale of
Ewyas and the country of great delight between the River
Trothy and the Monnow, are, in their solitude, apart from
the rest of the county. This is where the borders of Breck-
nock and Herefordshire are not far away, and towards
Monmouth one is getting near to Gloucestershire and the
Forest of Dean.

The alluvial coastal strip is another different type of
land. It differs in structure and wild life, and seems somewhat remote in its nearness to the channel, its flatness, and
its local titles of "The Marshes" and "The Moors".
Much of the county is made up of old red sandstone,
except for patches of alluvium in odd places along the
river banks and on the coast, and a strip of carboniferous
limestone which runs from around Magor, through
Chepstow, and into Gloucestershire. And in the west are
the great coalfields.

Although I am dividing the county up into "chapters",
it is likely that there will be no comprehensive study of
village by village and year by year. With history, people,
and nature as our guides, we cannot be tied down to a
card-index.

The county is not tremendous, which makes for a feeling of being at home in any part of it. In Newport, which
is probably like most other provincial towns in that
respect, "everyone knows everybody else", or almost!
Certainly not much escapes the notice of the native. This
feeling spreads throughout the county, though this is
divided to a certain extent into districts—much as I have
suggested for a "county plan". "The Valleys" are lumped
together to mean the industrial districts. If you live "up

The Sea Wall, Peterstone
The Severn Estuary, from Catsash

the Valleys" you are, in all probability, conversant with all the goings on in *all* the Valleys. The remote northern parts of the county are, perhaps, not quite in this "local" atmosphere; and it is easier, there, for Hereford to be used as a centre rather than Newport.

Newport is a clearing house for most of the county. She comes into contact with industry, because of the big works and the Docks; then there is the Cattle Market where the farmers come. Wednesday is a busy day in Newport, and if you happen to be around the bottom end of Dock Street, near the Cattle Market, or thereabouts, on that day of the week, it must not surprise you to see a herd of cows in the very urban streets.

Then there are the Monmouthshire people, past and present. History to me is not so much a succession of dates and dynasties, but rather a living thing. The air in our churches is full of the worship of countless generations; our chapels are sanctified by the past righteousness, and sometimes narrowness, of nonconformist enthusiasm. These people helped to shape the towns in which we live, and tended the fields that are still our heritage. Often vague where actual dates are concerned, when I see one of the old castles of which Monmouthshire has so rich a legacy, I am caught up in the atmosphere. Where so much history has passed within those thick walls, I have this feeling of the past and present mingling together in our lives, and I am able to imagine a pageant of people being loyal to their leaders, or traitors to their cause, and being lauded or punished in the manner of their day. Kings and barons and their retinue, citizens and villagers, by their laws, and the breaking of them, by their children's children, and those who came after them, have made us, to a certain extent, what we are today.

9

Caldicot Castle
Norman Arch, St Woollos, Newport

CHAPTER I

THE MARSHES AND THE MOORS

"The soile by south toward Severn is sumwhat low and fulle of dikes to drene it. Ther is lightly great plenty of benes, and in divers places it berith al other maner of corne."—John Leland (sixteenth century).

THE WENTLLWG LEVEL

ALONG the coast of Monmouthshire is a strip of alluvial land, turning to a type of marsh and moorland before rising to the more usual undulating country of the rest of the county. From the River Rhymney to the Usk it is known as the Wentllwg Level. The old Wentllwg spread along the banks of the Rhymney, but today the name is confined to the coastal strip below the Cardiff road. To enquire for "the marshes" would bring a quicker response, in these parts, than to ask for the Wentllwg Level. To say a person farms "down on the marshes" is sufficient to denote that he has a farm at St Bride's, the Duffryn, Coedkernew, or one of the other places on the Level. It is usually a case of farming, and not merely *living* on the marshes, for the main reason for having a house there at all is to carry on the business of farming. Many of the families have farmed on the marshes for generations.

Perhaps the name gives a mistaken air of complete desolation to this expanse of flat land which is, in fact, good pasture land. It is, I admit, a land apart, with its breath of the sea and its remoteness, and, in the winter, with a sharp, misty rain blowing, "the marshes" it is. Later in the year it takes on new colour with the yellow flags growing in the green reens which drain the meadows; and the little bridges cross to the farmhouse gates and into the flat fields made brighter by the sun. Moorhens jerk their way along through the undergrowth of the reens' banks, and there are usually a few farmhouse ducks swimming in the water.

I talk complacently of "reens", forgetting that this is rather a local name, and that many readers will not have come across reens in their own districts. Unless the district is flat it is unlikely that the land is crossed by these water-filled ditches, and I believe different parts of the country have their own names for them. The coast road is bordered by reens without any protective hedge or wall, and reens go across the fields to irrigate the land. Only in the flat coastal districts on both sides of the Usk estuary are reens found in Monmouthshire, and perhaps because this country is so unlike the rest of the county it has such a very different atmosphere. Some of the reens are fairly clear of vegetation, while others are packed with closely growing grass, sedge, and reeds, with sometimes a stunted bush or tree on the banks.

Places must be very like people. They have a character all their own, even if one does not happen to like that type of character. Likewise, one loves a friend, faults included, and so it is with a place: and some impeccable people are just like some places, there is not much character to find. The Wentllwg Level has character indeed, and I would say it is a strong one, but I find it a little difficult to get on with. There it is, that is just a matter of opinion, and there are parts of it I like very much. I like some of the names, too, names which associate themselves so much with the life that goes on around, such as Pheasant Bridge and Cuckoo Bridge—Pont-y-Cwcw—the improvident harbinger of spring singing the same song in any language.

This district should not be alien to me, because the first member of my family, originating in mid-Wales, came into Monmouthshire at the end of the seventeenth century, or beginning of the eighteenth, and settled on the marshes. The first of many of the family to be buried at Marshfield was Charles Phillips, son of the Vicar of Aberedw in Radnorshire, and he lived at Gelli-bêr and was Steward, after the death of Sir William Morgan in 1731, to Thomas, Sir William's brother and heir. There was always one member of the family farming on the marshes until fairly recent years, so I should have some affinity to the place.

The name of Morgan was bound to occur very soon in a book of Gwent. To delve deeply into the detailed history of the Morgan family is beyond my scope, as they originated, or so it seems, before any records were made. In his excellent book *Between Mountain and Marsh*, the late Antony Pickford traces the developments of the family as it spread about the county, particularly in the Rhymney Valley and Wentllwg. As he says in his book, "It was indeed Morgan country". Antony Pickford himself, had he lived, would have brought new honour to the county. He died in 1946, in his early twenties, having already added to the scholarship of the county he loved, apart from the great promise shown in his academiccareer.

Morgan must be one of the oldest names in Gwent. Angharad, the daughter of Sir Morgan ap Meredydd, married Llewelyn ap Ivor, Lord of St Clears. Sir Morgan ap Meredydd was a descendant of one of the oldest families in Gwent, in South Wales in fact. The pedigree of Meredydd Gethin, his great-grandfather, who built Castell Meredydd near Machen, can be traced back to the tenth century to Hywel Dda (Howell the Good), the

great Welsh law-maker and ruler of Wales. One son of
the marriage of Angharad with Llewelyn was Morgan,
and this was the beginning of the line of Morgan that
spread about the county, often cousin marrying cousin,
the estates growing. The main branch of Morgan is still
that of Tredegar. Throughout this book the name will
recur, because it is linked with the county's growth;
some of the family reached high office, others lived quiet,
country lives, just part of the pattern.

The family of Lewis, of St Pierre, near Chepstow, is a
Morgan offshoot, its age and fame running almost
parallel with the Morgans of Tredegar. The difference in
name occurs because Thomas (Thomas ap Lewis), a son
of Lewis (in his turn of the Morgan line), took his father's
name as his surname: this was at the time when surnames
were beginning to take the place of the involved "ap",
which could go on indefinitely through the generations.

Loyalty to the Crown appears to have been a strong
point with the Morgans (in fact, once the Border troubles
were settled, Gwent provided many loyal friends for the
cause of the Crown, as we shall see). During the Civil
War Sir William Morgan welcomed Charles I to Tredegar House on the 16th and 17th July, 1645, after Naseby.
Parliament must have been appeased in some way, for no
hardship befell the Morgans for their previous loyalty.

When the country had become more peaceful it was
decided that the Morgans of Tredegar should have a
residence in keeping with the splendour of so old a family.
By 1674 another Sir William had completed the re-
building of Tredegar House, the house as it stands today.
The old hall is all that remains of the old structure. The
first Viscount Tredegar told a meeting of the Cambrian
Association that, "A residence formerly stood on this

spot, which Leland mentioned as a 'fair place of stone'. Owain Glyndwr, when he ravaged Wentllwg and destroyed houses, churches, and Newport Castle, probably destroyed Tredegar House. On an inquisition being taken after this period of the value of the lordship, the return was NIL." Tredegar House is on the Wentllwg Level, not far from the River Ebbw; although it was built after the death of Inigo Jones, the design is said to be his, but this is improbable according to authorities on architecture. Sir William must have spent great wealth on the sumptuous rooms, the Grinling Gibbons carvings, and the spaciousness of the whole building.

Apart from the lesser-known Morgan families and the Tredegar Morgans (sometimes the inheritance going to a Machen brother or a Ruperra cousin or nephew), there were Morgans of Llantarnam, Llanrumney (the buccaneer, Sir Henry Morgan, of the seventeenth century, being one of these), Pencoed, and Bassaleg, to name a few. In 1382 Langstone Court, still standing in ancient isolation, was purchased for a second son of Morgan of Tredegar. So many of the estates were originated by Gavelkind, the law whereby each son received an equal share as his inheritance, and where expansion was impossible then the dividing-up of the existing estate took place.

In 1792 the line continued through a woman, Jane, who succeeded her brother, John. Her husband, Sir Charles Gould, took the name of Morgan when his wife inherited the estates, and their grandson became the first Baron Tredegar in 1859. Godfrey Charles, the first Viscount, was perhaps the real "character" among the Morgans. He lived in prosperous times, and took a great relish in all kinds of local affairs, especially agricultural shows and hunting, and he was the local Member of

Parliament. In his young days he took part in the famous and tragic Balaclava Charge. (And on the Marshfield road is a little inn called The Balaclava.)

His successor, his nephew, continued his uncle's pack of hounds, and the Boxing Day Meet at the Kennels was a social occasion for anyone who cared to be there—much more of a social engagement than a hunting one, I fancy, for everyone concerned, whether mounted on horse, bicycle, or following on foot. When Evan Morgan, his son, succeeded to the title, the pack was disbanded. Evan Morgan died in 1949; he was a poet, writing of spiritual things. A month or two ago* I could have written that Tredegar House was still occupied by a Morgan, though not in direct line. However, the now inevitable reasons of taxation and high costs have closed it, just as the Honourable John seemed to be getting into the local swing and affection. It is wrong that such a long connection is broken.

Most of the streets in Newport are still on Morgan land, unless they happen to belong to the Llanover and Llanarth Estates, but that is the commercial side of it. It is the idea that the beauty of past architecture should be allowed to deteriorate, and that the craftsmen's furniture should lie idle and unseen.

The low-lying fields of the marshes tend to flood in bad weather, but the flood which caused so much destruction, and has remained in history as the greatest recorded inundation of the Levels, was the one in 1606. It is chronicled that the coastline on both sides of the Bristol Channel was afflicted by a great tidal wave which swept over the villages, drowning many people and their livestock. St Bridget's Church at St Bride's Wentllwg had water to the depth of about five feet within its walls, and

* During 1950.

that church lies some way back from the sea. In the porch is a stone tablet recording the disaster which happened on the morning of the 20th January, 1606, and the wording on the tablet begins, "The great flvd 20 Janvarie in the morning 1606 . . .".

St Bride's Church, at the end of the lane, stands next to the Church House Inn, and quite close to the Rehobeth Chapel. Church House was the birthplace of one of the comparatively few Monmouthshire members of the acting profession, Lyn Harding. This lonely spot seems a strange backcloth for the upbringing of one who found his life among the bright lights of the theatre.

Considering the smallness of the village, the spiritual needs of the community are looked after very well, in more ways than one. This mingling of chapel and church (and the inn, of course) is noticeable in small villages all over the county, which seems to me to point to the double influence of England and Wales. Not, of course, that the denominations divide the English from the Welsh, but the chapels are mostly of Welsh bias, and their names are familiar—Horeb, Bethany, Ebenezer, Tirzah, to mention a few. The church is now administered by the Church in Wales, but its character is less Welsh than the chapel. It was not until 1920 that the Church became disestablished from the English Church. Nevertheless, Welsh was the language in most places of worship until the late nineteenth century.

Perhaps it was the flood that gave St Bride's Church the slant it has. Seen from any angle the tower has a decided list—but what a beautiful tower it is. On each of its four sides there is a carved figure in a niche, the female figure being St Bridget herself, presumably. The small, round turret surmounting the tower reminds me of a carved

16

pulpit set high above the congregation. The interior, in common with so many of our restored churches, is disappointing architecturally. The St Bride of the dedication is an anglicised version of Saint Fraid, more properly Saint Ffraed, an Irish saint who lived from 453 to 525. The village of St Bride's should, therefore, be called Llansantffraed. (The prefix "Llan" means a gathering place, or enclosure, indicating a church, and occurring so many times throughout the Principality.) There is such a name near Abergavenny, and there is St Bride's Netherwent on the Caldicot Level, so the saint was beloved in Gwent. There is a long story of Saint Ffraed in a delightful book, *The Heroines of Welsh History*, published in 1854, and written by T. J. Llleweyn Prichard. Several of the ladies of ancient Gwent are extolled in the book, and also many others of Welsh connection, including Mistress Eleanor Gwynn, whose career seems slightly at variance with the wording of the dedication, warm-hearted though she must have been:

To Virtuous Votaries
of
True Womanhood
in all
Its Graces, Purity, and Excellence, as Contra-distinguished from the Fantastic Fooleries and Artificial
Characteristics of
Fine Ladyism
in the Middle Walks of Life,
This Work is dedicated by their ardent admirer
The Author.

I am quite sure that Saint Ffraed fully deserved this exceptional praise.

2* 17

Allt-yr-yn

The other particularly graceful church tower along the coast is that at Peterstone Wentllwg. From a distance it stands up against the flat land like a cathedral. This church was built originally in 1142 and rebuilt in 1450, and again after the flood. The flood penetrated here more understandably, as the church is nearer the sea; it has become even nearer quite recently, when part of the shore fell into the sea. Sir Joseph Bradney tells of a rare pamphlet relating to the floods, when Mistress Van (daughter of John Morgan of Wentllwg Castle) was drowned at Gelli-bêr, Marshfield:

> "Moreover one Mistresse Van, a gentlewoman of good forte, whose living was an hundred pound and better by the yeare, is avouched before she could get uppe into the higher roomes of her house, having marked the approach of the waters, to have bene surprised by them and destroyed, howsoever, her house being distant above foure miles in breadth from the sea."

The old village pound is still marked by a sturdy boundary pillar in the churchyard beneath the neat tower at Marshfield. Towards Cardiff are St Mellons and Rumney, but they are now suburbs of Cardiff, and are little towns in their own right. Castleton is mostly old, but there is a newness creeping up from Marshfield, which hovers between the old and the new. Marshfield is "the marshes" still, but the others, though of the Wentllwg Level, can hardly be termed the marshes today.

When I was small we travelled down to the Lighthouse or Peterstone in the little Coastline Service 'buses, almost enough of us in one picnic party to fill the bone-shaking, box-like vehicle. We must have been a left-over from the enormous picnic parties which travelled in horse-brakes down to the coastline overlooking the Bristol Channel. Picnics *were* picnics then, not a snack in a paper bag. Even I have memories of whole cold chicken, a dozen hard-boiled eggs, trifle in a glass dish, and enough to eat to forget that one was sitting on a cliff or sea wall. The dining-room table must have been the only missing article.

Another pleasant pastime of the marshes was Knobblers. Knobblers was the name of the game and the name of the people who played it. It was, exclusively I believe, a summer game of a certain section of the Newport Rugby players, and their motto was "Sport Ever". I fancy the players must have cycled to the Lighthouse, St Bride's, or Peterstone, because in one contemporary photograph bicycle-clips, over tight Edwardian trousers, are a feature of the group. The only adaptation of everyday apparel appeared to be the removal of jackets; otherwise dress was formal for the game, including high, stiff, white collars. The basis of the game was the throwing of a stone at an eighteen-inch "tower" of stones. The rules seemed to be a variation of bowls, as the stones had to hit the target or fall closely to it. Simple enough, but popular while it lasted. Officially, I believe, this was not very long, but I have seen Knobblers played down on the marshes until just before the recent war, but mostly as a "round" or "family" game, and played under the guidance of an original "Knobbler".

Once a year the Newport Thursday Rugby XV played a football match against a Knobblers' XV, and in the "stone-throwers' " team came such internationally famous names as Walter Martin, C. M. Pritchard, T. H. (Tommy) Vile, and Reg. Plummer, Walter Martin and

Tommy Vile in their famous partnership. The Knobblers must have been a grand crowd, and in those days home-made entertainment still held first place in the social life of a town. After the Annual Rugby Match came the Dinner, the first of which was held in 1908. The menu held no surprises, but comprised good solid fare fit for men who worked and played hard. The choice of sweets on the menu showed some originality with "Knobbler Pudding" and "Sauce-à-la-Twyn-y-Pwll", "Crême-à-la-Church House", and "Reen Jelly" (I wonder if it was true to its name, and bright green in colour), and the simply named "Lighthouse Tarts".

The coastline of the marshes is Newport's "seaside", but in these days, when excursions to Barry Island or Porthcawl are in the common run of things, the Lighthouse and St Bride's are somewhat neglected, though in the last year or two there has been an attempt to put them on the map.

I believe the heron is becoming more scarce on the marshes, but there are plenty of more common birds there. Magpies are by no means scarce, and they seem particularly bold, as I have walked past them, within a yard or two, without disturbing them. One wet January afternoon a field near Peterstone was a black, moving carpet of birds. As one lot settled the birds farthest away flew over them, just above them, and came down on the near-side; then the farthest away again did the same thing. It was a moving, chattering carpet. The flock was mixed. The birds making the most chatter were starlings, but among them were a number of peewits, the plaintive cry sounding over the starlings' talk. When they flew, the white on their wings showed up clearly in the dull light. The flock of starlings grew as smaller flocks flew from behind the church from the direction of the sea, and they were also joined by one more flock of peewits, who flew in with their leisurely flapping of wings. The continuous motion brought the birds almost to the edge of the field; then they began to move in a similar manner in the opposite direction, until they were too far away to be seen in the fading light. The other fields around, and on the other side of the road, were empty of birds, save for an occasional pair of magpies.

The Castleton Beagles hunt across this land, and mostly run to earth in a cabbage field or a field under plough. For the followers this should be called "hedging and ditching" with no obstacles barred. As far as I can see, the afternoon's run seems more disturbing to the hare than dangerous.

From the coast to the main Cardiff road there is a slight gradient, and the country is less "marshy" and more undulating, and there are a few small copses as the ground rises. These do not amount to much, but I know the one near Tyn-y-Brŵyn causes a mild excitement when the point-to-point races are held there. The horses disappear around the wood, and until they reappear at the jumps before coming up the straight, no one has any idea which horse is winning. There are a few copses, and willows grow around the reens, and not many more trees of any size grow on the marshes.

THE CALDICOT LEVEL

Although the Caldicot Level is part of the Monmouthshire coastal strip, it has a subtle difference from the Wentllwg Level. I always feel a less bleak atmosphere in the Caldicot Level. "The moors" this land is called, although in parts it is of a similar nature to the marshes on the other side of the river. The old Welsh name is morfa-ddu—the black moor. As it leaves the coast, and also towards the east, its character varies, becoming more wooded and undulating: near Newport there is little difference from the Lighthouse area, save that industry has grown along the river bank. The hilly land around Llandevaud, or through Knollbury on to Common Coed, has a definite moorlike character, with its bracken and its open aspect. At one time the Forest of Wentwood stretched its woody fingers across what is now the main Newport to Chepstow road, and for that reason some of the places which appear to come in the Caldicot Level will not be visited until the Wentwood chapter, because they were outposts of the great forest, while their castles, some of which still remain, guarded the royal rights.

Like the whole of the Severn estuary, the Caldicot Level felt the force of the great seventeenth-century flood, and the threat of inundation has always been present, but now it is the Newport suburbs which encroach upon the moors; suddenly the creeping tide of modern dwellings ceases, and an occasional small farm-house is left in the flat expanse. The land here makes good pasture, and it seems more often than not one sees patches of flood-water: I have seen horses standing on the furrowed grass, with water in each channel, and last winter the swans came to rest on the waters of the floods.

The air at Goldcliffe has a decided "sea-breezes" heartiness, especially as the village is left behind and the right-angled road leads down to the sea-wall, which is very pleasant when there is a full tide and a stiff breeze. "Goldclift, singularly famous for its transparent shining Rocks and Clifts, and the gilded sands that lie about it",

22

wrote Nathan Rogers in the early eighteenth century. Goldcliffe does not appear to be as golden as that today, but it is pleasant enough. Apart from the farming on the good pasture land, fishing is one of the major industries in this rural area at the mouth of the Severn, at Goldcliffe, Porton, and Redwick, and other places along the coastline.

Recently there has been a change of detail in the salmon-fishing methods at Goldcliffe, which have remained otherwise unchanged for at least five hundred years. The wooden baskets, known as putchers, have been replaced by similar shaped wire baskets. The conical putchers are arranged on larch rails supported by stout poles in a long line across the Severn estuary; in fact, at Goldcliffe, in two lines, one with the open mouths of the baskets facing the outgoing tide, while the other line has the baskets facing down-stream, to catch any fish swimming in the opposite direction. The putchers are set at the beginning of the season, and not taken up again until the end (the season lasts from May until August); horses and carts are used to convey the baskets over the mud at low tide for this purpose, while at low tide during the summer months the baskets are emptied of their catch by the fishermen. The poles upon which the putchers are set are mostly of larch, and the present owner of the fishery, Mr Ralph Burge, says that one larch pole has been in existence, to his knowledge, for thirty years and, in his opinion, he believes the wood becomes pickled by the salt water.

The original line of putchers and poles dates back to 1442, when much of the land along the coast belonged to the foundation of Eton College. Henry VI, the founder of the College, decreed that a certain amount of the revenue from the land should provide for Masses to be said for him. Religion was the solace of this unfortunate son of Monmouth-born Henry V. Although five hundred years might seem a long time for an industry to carry on in much the same way throughout the ages, it is thought that the Romans fished at this point. It is certain that the sea-wall owes its original existence to them, as a stone set up by the Romans was found embedded in the wall in 1878, and this states that a certain length of the wall was indeed built by Roman soldiers.

Near the fishery is the highest part of the cliff at Goldcliffe, and on this "hill" was built a priory in 1113, founded by a Norman, Robert de Chandos. Today the only remains of the priory are in a barn of the farm which occupies the site. The priory was of the Benedictine Order, being a cell of the Abbey of Bec, and probably not very popular with the local Welsh. As an alien monastery Edward I seized Goldcliffe in 1285, and the lands were given to Tewkesbury Abbey. Later, when Henry VI founded Eton College, the lands were endowed to the foundation of the College, went back to Tewkesbury, and about the middle of the fourteenth century became, finally, part of the Eton endowment; this ownership did not cease until about 1920, and a little connection still remains: the College sends £2 a year to the village church school. The priory lands stretched beyond the limits of the present Goldcliffe parish to the eastwards and to Christchurch. Fresh water was brought down to the monks from Wentwood by means of some kind of medieval pipe-line, and one of the drainage gouts to the Severn is known as the Monk's Ditch.

The low-towered church at Goldcliffe was dedicated by its patron, Robert de Chandos, to a Norman saint—

St Mary Magdalene. The flood is graphically described on the memorial plate:

1606

ON THE XX DAY OF IANVARY EVEN AS IT CAME TO
PAS IT PLEASED GOD THE FLVD DID FLOW TO THE
EDGE OF THIS SAME BRAS AND IN THIS PARISH
THEARE WAS LOST 5000 AND OD POWNDS BESIDES,
XXII PEOPLE WAS IN THIS PARRISH DROWN

GOLDCLIF { JOHN WILKINS OF PIL REW AND
WILLIAM TAP CHURCH WARDENS

1609

The Severn has always played its part in the life of the moors in one way and another: making fertile farm land, giving anxiety before the land was reclaimed, bringing salmon to the fishermen—and smugglers on dark nights throughout the ages. As early as the fourteenth century the authorities were troubled by smugglers, and the eighteenth century showed the illicit traders at the peak of their activities. All the creeks (or Pills, as they are called along here), from the outskirts of Newport along to Chepstow, were used to bring contraband into Britain without paying any official Customs duties. A moonless night, the bleak, flat land, muffled oars, and the Severn estuary would be stirring with intrigue, while another cargo of spirits and tobacco from the Continent would be hidden in a farm outbuilding on the moors.

One surreptitious crossing of the Severn at New Passage was during the Civil War, when King Charles, after a short stay at Crick, ferried from Black Rock to the Gloucestershire shore to escape from Cromwell's soldiers. Very little is known of this flight, nor of the crossing when a party of Ironsides were drowned. Presumably these were the soldiers who were pursuing Charles. The ferrymen were Royalists, and took the soldiers as far as the un-covered English Stones, telling them it would be necessary for them to walk the rest of the way owing to the low tide. They did not tell the soldiers that the tide would soon be over the English Stones, cutting off the land and all means of salvation. Archdeacon Coxe puts forth the view that as a result of this incident the ferry was closed down, and not reopened until 1718, while others say that Charles's crossing was merely intended and never carried out.

There is a smell of the sea at Black Rock, where sea-weed covers the rocks, and the lighthouse on Charston Rock heightens the illusion; though at one time Charston was joined to the mainland.

Not far from Black Rock, near Portskewett, is the one end of a very different kind of river crossing, the Severn Tunnel. The pumps and maintenance works rise un-expectedly on the coast besides the Iron Age camp at Sudbrook, while in the long terrace of houses dwell the workers who keep the Tunnel in order for the underwater journey of four miles six hundred and twenty-four yards, of trains on the line from South Wales to the Gloucester-shire side of the Severn, the link between South Wales and Paddington. I always think of Paddington as the most intensely regional of the main stations in London. During the war particularly there was no need to ask if the train standing at No. 1 Platform was the 5.55 p.m. to South Wales, for the majority of the uniformed passengers spoke with the voice of home.

During the construction of a ferry serviced by the old Bristol and South Wales Union Railway at New Passage, the engineer, Charles Richardson, saw the possibilities of a tunnel beneath the river, but it was not until 1872 that the Act was passed permitting the Great Western Railway

THE MARSHES AND THE MOORS

Company to begin operations. In 1873 the work commenced, under the direction of Charles Richardson, and things went fairly smoothly until 1879, when the partly constructed tunnel was flooded. This was a great blow to Mr Richardson, who had always been so certain that the structure of the river-bed was such that he need fear no flooding from the Severn. However, the water flooding the tunnel turned out to be clear, and unlikely to be river water. The unforeseen had happened, and the excavations had touched a land spring, known thereafter as the Big Spring or the Great Spring.

At this time the Engineer-in-Chief of the Railway Company, Sir John Hawkshaw, took over direction of the work, with T. A. Walker, a well-known engineering contractor, in a superior position to that of Charles Richardson. In later years, in letters and papers read to certain engineering societies, Richardson indicated his resentment of the prominence given to Mr Walker as the engineering brain behind the Tunnel project, and also some of the statements made in T. A. Walker's book, particularly as without those first thoughts back in 1862, and the struggle to bring the scheme to the notice of Parliament, there would have been no Tunnel. Even so, both men must have been brilliant engineers when one considers the result, and without knowing more personal history an impartial view must be held.

After the flooding by the Big Spring, and the resultant prevention of such an occurrence again, the work went on with periods of success and incidents of disappointment for fourteen years. The Tunnel was completed in April 1885, and three months later a train ran through, but everything was not quite in order. It was finally opened for passenger service in July 1887. Over 3,500 men were

27

employed on the construction of the Tunnel; it is venti-
lated by a fan some forty feet in diameter, and the foul air
is disgorged through a shaft at Sudbrook. T. A. Walker,
in later years, lived at Mount Ballan, a little above
Caldicot, and not far from his achievement.

Both Portskewett and Sudbrook are ancient places.
Various spellings have superseded the present-day "Portskewett" (Porth is Coed, Portascyth, Portscwit), but the
meaning has derived from "Harbour under the wood",
indicating the importance of the place as a port in far-off
days, possibly being the landing-place of the Romans
coming to Caerwent.

The Long Barrow at Portskewett and the Camp at
Sudbrook are proof of early occupation. The Barrow is
known as Harold's Tump, but while Harold did have a
residence of some kind at Portskewett, the Barrow is of
much earlier date, though a later building could have been
set upon it. Harold's presence evidently was not welcomed
by the Welsh, as in 1065 his house, hunting lodge, or
castle, was destroyed, some saying that it was still in
preparation and that his workmen were slain while the
building was demolished.

The Lewis family of St Pierre acquired half the manor
of Sudbrook when, in 1526, Henry Lewis married the
daughter of the manorial lord, and she inherited a half-
portion. In 1587 Thomas Lewis of St Pierre purchased the
manor of Portskewett.

I suppose "homely" is the description of the villages
on the moors—among them Nash, with its church pews
closed in by high doors, Undy, Redwick, Wilcrick, and
St Bride's Netherwent. There seem so many villages on
this side of the river compared with Wentllwg; there are
Llandevenny, Whitson (with its ancient pinnacled square

28

church tower), and many more. Very few of the Monmouthshire villages are architecturally exciting. They are
neat, and often pleasant, but there is none of the mellow
beauty of the actual buildings which is found in every
Cotswold village. The really pretty village is the exception in Gwent, particularly in the south. Of course, there
are the sudden flashes of beauty in a cottage with an old-
fashioned garden, or a church set in trees, and the down-
to-earth satisfaction of most villages. This is real farmland, with the meadows patched with cowslips in the
spring. Between Llanwern and Whitson, in May, the
whole air is laden with the scent of white may-blossom. It
is the country itself that holds the charm. I am not saying that there are no beautiful villages in Monmouthshire
—there are, really delightful ones, but they are not the
general rule.

Set well alone on the moors, close to the coast, is
Redwick with its immaculate cottages and farms. The
church, with one of the few remaining rood screens in the
county, has been restored almost out of existence. The
little of the screen that remains has been painted with
some sort of varnish.

Some of the land around Redwick, and in other parts
of the moors, is used by farmers in the hilly land farther
north as meadowland. I know it is not uncommon for
cattle to be walked twenty-five miles to graze for a
fattening period on land rented for the purpose.

Llanwern is one of those places which is almost
touched by Newport now, and there are new houses, but
it still remains part of the moors. The church, from the
outside, has an appearance of neglected age. There is a
string of villages along the moors, and a "businessman's
train" in the morning stops at each one to pick up the

town's workers. All along this line are the distinctive square-towered churches. Magor is one of the line of villages, and a pleasant place it is. The ruins adjoining the church are of great age; the church was founded in the seventh century by Cadwaladr, but for all that the chapel in Magor plays quite a large part in the life of the village, and at Whitsuntide the children of the village walked in procession through the little square and into the chapel, each carrying a circlet of flowers, which were hung on the walls until they became walls of flowers.

Roggiett, the village Severn Tunnel has turned into a miniature Swindon, is rather out of place among the string of villages, with its rows of houses and railway lines. The old village adjoins the Junction. Within a very short distance is Llanvihangel-near-Roggiett, also with its square-towered church, and both churches are set almost in two farmyards, Llanvihangel having no real road to it save the pathway through an old-fashioned farmyard, with fine fowl drinking from a stone trough and walking with stout dignity up the barn steps. Both these churches have a similarity, being small and unadorned, and they date back to the twelfth century. In Llanvihangel there is an ancient font, of heavy stone, with no carving. It is much lower than the more usual font on a pedestal, and the stone plinth is of much more recent date, and I should imagine it to be prior to the twelfth century. There is not a great deal of personal record in the churches, but there are two rather defaced effigies at Llanvihangel, the best preserved being that of the woman, Anne Martel, who died about 1270, and the other a man, probably her husband, John, who both lived in the parish.

Probably the biggest events on the moors today are connected in some way with rural life, but at one time

Bishton, little Bishton today, and Mathern were centres of great ecclesiastical scenes. Both were residences of the Bishops of Llandaff, more especially after Owain Glyndwr had destroyed the main residence, Llandaff Castle. Mathern became the favoured residence and was so, in fact, until the eighteenth century. Bishton, or Bishopston, was known as Llangadwaladr, presumably having been founded, like Magor, by the last Prince of Wales who was also a King of Britain, Cadwaladr.

Mathern Palace, in its secluded site, retains some of its old splendour, while the whole village, some way from the ancient houses connected with the church, is clean and neat, with a cheerfulness about it. The trees are noble in the fields; this part of the Level, St Pierre Park, Wye-lands, and Mathern, has many great trees, individual trees rather than woodland, and mainly oak and chestnut. Before the land turns down towards the church and the palace there is a big Tudor house, now a farm, called the Innage, and that, too, has an ecclesiastical look about it.

If such a thing can be said about a church, I would say the one at Mathern is just right. The interior stonework is well tended and, like the village, it has a brightness, it is cared for. I went in one Saturday afternoon, after a mid-week harvest festival, and all the flowers and produce were still there, to last over the Sunday services. Trails of berries wound around the lectern, dahlias filled the window-sills, and Michaelmas daisies were bunched everywhere. A great cottage loaf and a miniature haystack stood on the altar steps, while at the back of the nave were a row of vegetables and two mossy nests full of brown eggs. The place was alive with the glory of harvest. I thought there was no more space for another flower, but the sexton told me he had seen it better—when each

31

pillar had been decorated! Sometimes our churches have
a deadness about them; history is there, but not much
present worship to continue the story, but at Mathern
there is love, I am sure.

Worship has been going on for a long time at Mathern.
In the chancel is a large stone tablet telling the story of an
ancient martyr, and of the foundations of the church:

"Here lyeth the body of Theodorick, King of Mor-
ganuck commonly called St Thewdrick, and accounted
a Martyr, because he was slain in battle against the
Saxons, being then Pagans, and in defence of the
Christian religion. The battle was fought at Tintern,
where he obtained a great victory, but died here, being
in his way homeward, three days after the battle, having
taken order with Maurice his son, who succeeded him
in the kingdom, that in the same place he should
happen to decease, a church should be built and his
body buried in the same, which was accordingly performed in the year 600."

The ground was consecrated, and a church has stood on
this place from that time. The body of the martyr lies
under a stone slab near the tablet, which was erected in
the early years of the seventeenth century by Bishop Godwin. The arches along the nave are Norman, with the
exception of one, which is Saxon, so presumably Tewdrick did not die in vain.* In Pwll-Meyric the name of
Tewdrick's son, Meurig, is perpetuated. Perhaps Pwll-
Meyric was the last halt of the dying King of Morganwg
on his way from Tintern, before he was carried to his last
resting-place at Mathern. He must have been near to the

* The Rev. E. T. Davies, now Vicar of Llangibby, suggests in his Mathern
parish history this is local patriotism : the arches are probably thirteenth century
and Norman, not Norman and Saxon.

Canal bank, Allt-yr-yn

end then, for the two villages are not more than a mile apart.

Leading from one of the gates in the churchyard wall are large stone steps, shallow, but very wide, and these are moss-covered now and little used. They lead to a field where, if you are lucky, you might see a red squirrel run up one of the great trees. At the top of the field is Moynes Court, a house built even before Bishop Godwin counted it as one of his residences in the first decade of the seventeenth century. For a village so quiet today, Mathern has such lovely old buildings, of some splendour, and it must once have seen a certain grandeur that we do not know. Another very near neighbour is St Pierre, home of the Lewis family, already mentioned as being part of the Morgan pedigree. This is a fine house with an ancient Gate Tower, spacious parkland, and a big lake. It takes its name from the Norman family who settled in the district soon after the Conquest; today the house is used as a training centre for youth leaders.

In 1857, Charles Lewis of St Pierre purchased from the Crown the manor of Caldicot, including the castle, and since then it has been in possession of various private persons, and although there are records of the castle having fallen into decay, it is today inhabited, and has a wonderfully authentic atmosphere. So many of our castles are ruined, and, while portions here and there are sufficiently intact to give an idea of medieval life, Caldicot is still part of that life; or, at least, that is the impression I have. It is a big castle, and has many fine angles from which to see it, but the way I like best is to come down from Caerwent and see it ahead, the Woodstock Tower looking like an illustration from an old story.

The castle was built on what was probably a fortified

3
33

mound of some antiquity. The manor of Caldicot was held in the twelfth century by Milo Fitz-Walter, son of Walter Fitz-Roger, and grandson of the Lord High Constable of England. The earliest existing part of the castle, the keep, dates back to this period, but the greater part of the building was done by the de Bohuns. Milo Fitz-Walter's daughter, Margaret, married Humphry de Bohun. She inherited the Caldicot estates, and this was the beginning of the line of de Bohun which lasted for two hundred years. An influential family in Norman England, the de Bohuns were Earls of Hereford, Constables of England, and, with other powerful barons, curbed the influence of the Crown to a certain extent. Another Humphry married Edward I's daughter. By 1372 there was no male heir of the de Bohuns, and two little girls, Alianore, aged seven, and Mary, three years old, were left as wards of the Crown. Edward III settled the estates upon his youngest son, Thomas of Woodstock, until the little girls should come of age. Thomas did not waste much time, for within five years he had married Alianore; he was made Earl of Buckingham and later became Duke of Gloucester. The Gatehouse was built by Thomas, and, of course, the Woodstock Tower with its pinnacle. Mary, the other sister, married a grandson of Edward III, Henry Bolingbroke (later Henry IV), whose father was John of Gaunt, Duke of Lancaster. The son of Mary and Henry became Henry V—Prince Harry of Monmouth—and apart from the fact that he was born at Monmouth, his parentage gave him added allegiance to Gwent, although his blood was Norman, not Welsh. The white swan with a crown about its neck was a de Bohun device, and this was part of Henry V's insignia.

During the Wars of the Roses the castle changed

hands, inevitably, when the whole of the Border was in such a state of uncertainty, though remained part of the Duchy of Lancaster until the Civil War, when it was confiscated by Oliver Cromwell. At the restoration of Charles II it came back into the Duchy, until, in 1857, the manor came into private ownership. All the people who have owned Caldicot and lived within its fortified walls have given the old castle its atmosphere. The Keep, with its black dungeons: what a horrible form of torture that must have been. I have looked into the black depths of the dungeon beneath the Keep—no glimmer of light, no means of escape, just a small hatch, wide enough to allow the prisoner to be dropped through. The curtain walls were built in the de Bohuns' time, and Thomas of Woodstock built much of the existing structure. Then there is the Tudor influence, quite noticeable, with the much more "domestic" trend compared with the previous fortified building.

It might have nothing to do with ancient history, but I always think of Caldicot as the village with the delightfully named inn—The Tippling Philosopher.

Not much more than a mile from the medieval history book of Caldicot castle is Caerwent, a chapter in the history of the Roman occupation of Britain. Built not as a military fort, but as a civil town, the Romans were at Caerwent from about A.D. 73 to 425. Civil town or designated military fortress, defence was necessary in those days, and an earthen ramp was built on the inside of the town walls, and a ditch was made on the outside of the walls. The fierce Silures caused a certain amount of trouble before they were wooed over to the luxury of Roman life. Caerwent became the home of the Silures from the great hill-fort at Llanmelin, which lies between

Llanfair Discoed and Dinham, on the rising ground from Caerwent. An early Iron Age fort, Llanmelin has been excavated and found to contain various bones, both human and domestic animal, together with bronze, decorated bracelets, pottery, and metal objects.

The Silures lived in the town, governed by the Romans, and Caerwent was the administrative centre of Britannia Secunda, the South Wales area. An old history book gives a description of Roman occupation in Britain which could well apply to Caerwent:

"During the following Winter Agricola's chief Business was to soften the rough Manners of the Britons, and instill into them a Desire to imitate the Customs of the Romans. His Pains are not bestow'd in vain. Soon after, Britain is adorn'd with stately Temples, noble Porticos, and many fine structures, both publick and private, of a very different Taste from what had been hitherto seen. The British Nobles even pride themselves in speaking the Latin Tongue, to which a little before they were utterly averse. They dress likewise after the Roman manner, and in short, as Tacitus observes, are brought to esteem, as Politeness and good Breeding, what was only a Badge of their Slavery."

I think George Borrow, in his tour through Wales in 1854, was a little hard on Caerwent, unless, of course, it has improved very considerably. He dismisses it quite quickly.

"I passed through Caer Went, once an important Roman station, and for a long time after the departure of the Romans a celebrated British city, now a poor desolate place consisting of a few old-fashioned houses

36

and a strange-looking dilapidated church. No Welsh is spoken at Caer Went, nor to the east of it, nor indeed for two or three miles before you reach it from the west. The country between it and Chepstow, from which it is distant about four miles, is delightfully green, but somewhat tame."

Today Caerwent is a village of old and new built within the Roman walls, and with foundations of Roman building mingling with the later erections. New excavations are going on, while sheep crop the grass around the ancient walls. I never feel that Caerwent is at all conscious of its antiquity. One just wanders around to see the excavations, and a Roman wall is likely to be alongside the road as a normal boundary.

Even within the church at Caerwent, with its ancient large font and beautiful pulpit dating back to 1632, the Roman era is found mingling with the Christianity of a later age. In the porch are stone tablets bearing clear-cut lettering, while in a niche in the wall of the nave is an urn containing the bones and ashes of a Roman. St Tathan of Caerwent, who died in 590, is buried in the church: he made Caerwent an ecclesiastical centre, and his teachings were known throughout Gwent, and probably beyond, and he was head of a monastic "school". From the sixth century there was an Abbot of Caerwent, and about 1070 the first incumbent was appointed. Samuel Alsop, who held the living in 1649, was ejected in favour of Hopkin Rogers, who conformed to the ideas prevalent at that time. He, in his turn, was ejected at the Restoration.

There are only traces today of the past splendour of the moors.

37

CHAPTER II

NEWPORT

"It is a long, narrow, and straggling town, built partly in a flat
on the banks of the Usk, and partly on a declivity. The streets are
dirty and ill paved. . . . Notwithstanding its trade and situation,
the population is very inconsiderable. It contains only 221 houses
and tenements, and 1,087 souls."—Rev. William Coxe, from *A
Historical Tour through Monmouthshire,* 1801.

"The County Borough of Newport is one of the most extensive
ports on the Bristol Channel and the largest and most important
town in the County . . . it has an extent of 7,873 acres and a
population of 101,000." (From the current Official County
Guide.)

NEWPORT is home to me. Familiarity, far from breeding contempt, has bred in me an affection for the town,
perhaps to the extent of overlooking certain faults. The
welcome of old friends, the memories of past events, even
the little failures and heartaches, all go for a comfortable
affection. The town itself is industrial, yet there is never
far to go for a breath of fresh air. Most Newportonians
have an accent that is Welsh—until you hear a Welshman talk. "Newport Welsh"—and it is surprising the
number of local people who erroneously think they have
no accent at all: it is there in many of us whether we like it
or not. Our pronunciation of Welsh words is usually
atrocious, and surprisingly few people speak the Welsh
language.

There is no "olde worlde" beauty in Newport, none of
the normal characteristics of a market town, although it
is an agricultural centre as well as an industrial one. Dock-
land and industry, and lovely surrounding countryside—

38

those are Newport's contrasts, with a busy town built up mainly when industry was growing quicker than any planning could cope with, and the town becoming a county borough in 1891.

Like most provincial towns it is the people who make its life, not the big impersonal works, nor the amount of traffic which passes through its busy streets, but the familiar names, the shop on the corner, letters to the local Press—and the local Press itself. It is the reading between the lines in the *South Wales Argus* that makes it so much more personally interesting (and often more exasperating) than the national dailies. Each evening there are photographs of someone who is known throughout the town, or lives next door; or a paragraph relating to an old friend, somebody's cousin, or a dinner attended by all the local "personages".

The prosperity of Newport appears, during history, to have been a thing of fluctuation. In the Middle Ages it was prosperous, then it seemed to become almost non-existent, probably after the destruction caused by Owain Glyndwr. There was enough of the castle there, however, for a force of Royalists to hold out against Cromwell's men during the Civil War. By the sixteenth century the shipping trade was beginning to grow, and Leland said, "Newport is a bigge towne, whereof that parte where the paroche chirche stondith on a hille". With the natural resources that were too good to be missed by industrial development, Newport and district were caught up in the tide of industry by the early nineteenth century. This, of course, was happening everywhere during the nineteenth century, but the famous ironworks in the county, the new docks, and coal-mining, made the area one of tremendous activity in a comparatively short space of time.

In the first years of the nineteenth century Newport must have been in one of its doldrums, according to the writings of one, E. Donovan, F.L.S., who wrote in 1804:

"The interior of the town, however, disappointed us. Most of the houses are very mean, the streets ill-paved, and what is worse, remarkably dirty. Newport arose in consequence, on the decay of Caerleon, being stationed more conveniently for trade and lying some miles nearer to the Bristol Channel than the latter; but in its turn, Newport has given place to Cardiff, of which it is at this time considered only as a subordinate port."

Very little of historical interest has remained at Newport itself, although the outskirts are so deeply concerned with the past. Probably that is why the town failed to impress the early nineteenth-century traveller. The new town was not yet built, and there was little of history left: not much respect was shown to the little that still stood. The castle, which had played its part in the usual Border troubles, the Wars of the Roses, and the Civil War, was used, at the time Donovan wrote, as a tanner's yard.

St Woolos Church, Leland's "paroche chirche", stands high above the town at the top of Stow Hill, and is perhaps the best preserved historical building in Newport. The original religious site dates back to the early years of Christianity, but today the beautiful interior Norman work and Roman-style pillars are the features of the church. St Gwynllyw—St Woolos. St Gwynllyw is the name from which St Woolos comes, Gwynllyw having been the bold, bad son of a Lord of Wentllwg. He founded the church in the sixth century after a dream and consequent remorse. Part of the present building dates back to 1120, although it is likely that the outer walls of

40

St Mary's Chapel are pre-Norman. Perhaps the most beautiful stonework in St Woolos is the Norman archway leading from this chapel into the nave.

When Owain Glyndwr sacked the town and castle of Newport, the church at Stowe, upon the hill, was not overlooked, and it, too, was partially destroyed. The main part of the present building was begun in 1440, and Jasper Tudor was responsible for much of the work, including the heightening of the tower. The statue in the niche in the face of the tower is thought to be Jasper Tudor, whose stone figure was beheaded by Cromwell's men. Cromwell followed, with a couple of centuries between, in the wake of the other man of single purpose, Glyndwr, adding a little more destruction to one of the Welshman's victims, or finding a fresh building to mutilate.

Crindau House and the Murenger House are the only other buildings of any antiquity in the town itself. The Murenger is now an unusual combination of an open-all-day "eating house" and a normal pub, for want of a better description. The house lies in the busy High Street, its Tudor gable jutting out incongruously from its more recent neighbours. The Murenger was an official who collected the tolls used for the repair of the town walls, but the office died out in 1324. It seems, therefore, that the present building carried on the name the older foundation bore. I do not know why the Murenger House should have been spared while its contemporaries have become part of the dust of ages, but it does help to prove that Newport had an existence before the Industrial Revolution.

One of the members of the Herbert family lived in the Murenger House in the sixteenth century. The manor house of the Herberts was St Julian's, which was

demolished less than twenty years ago to make room for
modern houses. The Herberts were also the governors of
Newport Castle for some two hundred years, during which
time Colonel Herbert was forced to surrender it to the
Parliamentary forces. The Herberts were to be found all
over Gwent, and the most famous branch of the family
was the one at Raglan, and when Raglan Castle comes
into the story of Gwent the Herberts will take their
colourful place. There were Herberts of Troy, Abergavenny, Wonastowe, Caldicot, Coldbrooke, Usk Castle,
and many other places, so we are bound to meet them
again. The families of Herbert and Morgan were united
in marriage in several generations, and between them
covered the whole of the county.

We learn of numerous Herberts and Morgans
throughout the years, yet what of the many who for some
reason of obscurity or illegitimacy are not known to
posterity? The population was not great, and it makes me
think that the county must have been one vast family,
with few outsiders!

In Newport there was the main family at St Julian's,
and one, Sir William Herbert, must have been exceptionally proud of his name. He died in 1592 or 1593, and his
daughter would inherit certain lands, after the death of
her mother, on condition that,

"If it shall happen that she doe marry or take to
husband any other person then shalbe a gentleman of
my Sirname Herbert Then I give and bequeathe all
my lands tenements and hereditaments whatsoever
within the County of Monmouthe immediately after
the deathe of Dame fflorence my wife to William
Herbert eldest sonne of my uncle Miles Herbert and
to the heires male of his bodye lawfully begotten."

This goes on that in the default of any "heires male" the estates shall pass to some other male Herbert kin, and so on. There is one clause that if Dame fflorence herself should wed it must be to one of the Herbert surname, or else the estates would pass on, as indicated. Each bequest is made out in a similar manner. In fact, Sir William's daughter married her cousin, Lord Herbert of Cherbury, scholar, poet, and astronomer, and one-time ambassador to France.

Another sixteenth-century member of the family was George Herbert of the Murenger House, Newport, the second son of Sir Walter Herbert of St Julian's. He sounds a much more genial character, and left his goods and chattels to a variety of people. He was also a public benefactor. His will, made in 1580, after the usual acknowledgments, begins, "I give and bequeath towards the buylding of the Bridge of Newport aforesaid the somme of xl^{li} whereof there is alreadye paide to the Common Attourneys Harrye Johnes Rychard Morys and to Lewes Thomas xx^{li}". He also left to a brother his ship called "the greene Dragon with all her ffurniture and Tacklinge Ordinaunces shotte and poulder armour and munition" and "to Myles my Bark called the Stephen". This sounds Elizabethan and colourful. The *Green Dragon* and the *Stephen* must have looked very grand riding the tide at Newport.

Many of Newport's old buildings were pulled down at the end of the eighteen-nineties, and during the first decade of the present century, to make room for the road-widenings and general layout of the Newport of today.

Although the Chartist Riots were part of a great national unrest, they were, in themselves, practically a local event. The only other centre where there was any real trouble was Birmingham, and there it appears that the police and troops were the first to become aggressive. Newport was the scene of the riot, but the Valleys played their part in providing the men for the march. The Corn Laws were the breaking point of the surge of bitterness being experienced all over the country, but beneath this particular grievance were the much deeper needs of the people agitated by the usual political troubles. The People's Charter of 1838 set out the requirements, and it was the agitation for this Bill to be passed in Parliament which led to the Chartist movement. The six points in the Charter were Annual Parliaments, Universal Manhood Suffrage, Payment of M.P.'s, Votes by Ballot, Equal Electoral Districts, and Abolition of the Property Qualifications for Members of Parliament.

Although there was need for great improvement in the life of the working people in the early nineteenth century many of those who took part were agitators, not generally in favour with the more solid inhabitants; there is no doubt that the unrest was there, but agitation, usually from outside sources, brought with it the violence needed to gather together the rioters.

Earlier in the eighteen-thirties there had been the organisation, if such it can be called, known as the Scotch Cattle. These men attacked any workers who accepted lower rates of pay; they were violent towards the workers who went against their way of thinking, going so far as to destroy their homes and to cause them bodily harm, once fatally injuring a man at Blackwood. In Nantyglo and the Pontypool district they had also been particularly active, united under their emblem of a red bull's head. One writer who remembered the activities of the Scotch Cattle wrote in an account entitled "The last 30 years in a Mining District":

"The deeds of these barbarians were marked by one strange anomaly, the origin of which I never heard. If they entered a house, it was not to pillage, but to terrify its inmates, and before leaving they broke every single article of furniture: none was left unbroken, even to the fire-irons; but if there happened to be bread on the table, the table and bread were left untouched. It was considered sacrilege, and scrupulously to be avoided, the touching either the food (no matter what straits they were reduced to), or the furniture on which it rested, or the cupboard in which it was placed. Some short time before the murder just related at Blackwood, to such a pass had the scotchings arrived, that, at Blaina Iron-works, a company of foot and troop of horse were maintained for a considerable time."

The whole land was changing too rapidly. Towns were growing, works were being built, men—and women too —were being exploited, the whole structure of social life was disrupted. There was bound to be trouble of some sort. Because the problems were causing thought everywhere in Great Britain I do not want to go into the rights and wrongs of anyone concerned with the political movements of the nineteenth century, but I want to relate what happened when the Chartists of Monmouthshire marched upon Newport on the night of Sunday, the 3rd November, 1839.

According to all reports the night was dark and stormy, and there must have been a great stir throughout the Valleys as the various groups assembled and began to

march—from Blackwood, from Nantyglo, and from
Pontypool, led by John Frost (Mayor of Newport in
1836), Zephania Williams, and William Jones. A little
dull light must have been forcing through the clouds by
the time two of the columns met at Risca and were
marching upon Newport, sodden with rain, the powder
wet in the few muskets which strengthened the more
general weapons, which were pikes. The contingent
under William Jones had failed to complete the journey.
Led by John Frost, the remainder of the rebels crowded
upon the Westgate Hotel, where they had heard some of
their members were held prisoner. Behind the windows
of the hotel hid the forewarned troops and Sir Thomas
Phillips, Mayor of Newport, and as the rebels rushed at
the hotel the soldiers opened surprise fire. The Chartists
lost about fourteen of their men, and probably fifty were
wounded; the three leaders were eventually tried and condemned to death for treason, although later this sentence
was changed to deportation. Gwyn Jones, whose writing
takes its best form in short stories, wrote a play, *The Rock
and the Fountain*, for the centenary of the Riots, and
appropriately enough he is from Blackwood, one of the
centres of the rising.

The Chartist Riots are always mentioned in connection
with Newport as though they were the only historical
event ever to happen, just as everyone has to see the bullet
holes which remain in the pillars of the Westgate Hotel
doorway from that miserable early morning scene in
1839.

Something like one hundred years later, when the
industrial districts had grown through their early teething
troubles, reached a successful peak, and had begun a
downward trend again, South Wales was again in a bad

state. In the nineteen-thirties I can remember going from the centre of the town through Commerical Street and Commercial Road to the Docks and seeing empty shop after empty shop, the windows boarded up and dirty, the old posters, ragged, still stuck inside them, advertising cigarettes or chocolates that had long gone from the shelves inside. I was too young to understand that the prosperity of Newport was bound up with the Docks and industry throughout South Wales. That is, too, why this chapter has so much of the Valleys in it; Newport cannot be cut off from the rest of the county. There is life again, but always Newport's fortunes depend upon coal and the Docks, and the heavy industries, though the new industries might prevent such a gloom descending once more.

The town lies on both sides of the River Usk, and when the works were built in the Corporation Road and Somerton areas the Transporter Bridge was erected so that the workers living in the older Pill district, on the opposite side of the river, could cross the water without having to go the long distance to the main bridge. Liswerry was then used as a building site, and the Transporter became Newport's famous white elephant. For sixpence one could walk over the top of the bridge, and for one penny a ride in the suspended tram obtained. I do not know what has happened to the "over-the-top" fare, but it now costs nothing to go on the little tram, which to me, at one time, was a rather exciting experience, like going on to a ship: and there was the thrill of seeing a big ship come down to Cashmore's Yard on its last sad journey to be broken up. Until the advent of the works on the Nash side of the river, the town was centred mainly on the west bank of the Usk. The first substantial bridge to

47

be erected was in 1800, which lasted until 1927, when the present one was officially opened.

The main industries of Newport and district are the heavy industries, including the famous Whitehead group and the Lysaght connections. It is through the fame of companies such as these, old family businesses which have grown to world-wide renown, that Newport is thought of as a purely industrial town.

Then there are the Docks. Shipping in the Usk goes back over the ages, when ships sailed right up to Caerleon, and even to Newbridge-on-Usk. The old Town Dock was opened in 1842, but later it came under the ownership of the Alexandra (Newport and South Wales) Docks and Railway Company, which was incorporated in 1865. In 1902 the whole concern was taken over by the Great Western Railway Company.

The North Dock of the Alexandra Dock was opened in 1875, and the South Dock in 1894, while the additions went on, making Newport Docks very fine indeed. The entrance lock is 1,000 feet long by 100 feet wide. There is a deep-water area of $123\frac{3}{4}$ acres, which makes this one of the largest stretches of lock water in the world, and certainly the locking system is one of the best in the United Kingdom.

Wherever there are docks with the coming and going of foreign vessels there is the influx of various nationalities, some staying in the town for the duration of their ship's stay, and others settling down in the town, and making their homes in the dock area. A string of little Indians in round caps is a regular sight in the town when a ship is in, and groups of seamen of other nationalities advertise the docking of their vessels.

Newport has many old Devonshire families connected

48

Mountain road, Twyn Barllwm

with shipping in one way and another, often as pilots, and they live in houses which have been given the names recalling their native county.

It might be the lure of foreign lands, of the unknown, that makes a skyline of coal hoists and ships' funnels so fascinating. Down-river from Newport bridge there is a fine distance in the view; and walking down Commerical Street on a clear morning, with the Transporter Bridge way up and a long way ahead, there is that feeling of distances and the sea beyond.

Inside the Dock Gates, where rails cross and recross the roads, there is a feeling of aloofness for the stranger. The dockers are busy, the cranes swing around impersonally; the blond first-mate from a Scandinavian vessel is on his way to his ship, and a swarthy Portuguese is leaving for town. It is a world of its own within the gates, where little rowing boats lie on the mud of the river and a few houses are scattered about here and there. The coal trucks stand in the sidings, and coal is being loaded on to a collier:

> Her bow is to the east'ard,
> Lying right for coaling;
> And coal in clouds goes groaning
> Down to hungry holds.*

The international flavour of the Docks overflows into Commercial Road and all the streets around, and there is no doubt that the Docks are very much part of Newport. And when depression hits industry, then the Docks lie idle too. All the way down the river are wharves belonging to timber companies and scrap-iron merchants. There is a sub-post-office towards the Docks (and there are shops

* John K. Kennedy, from "Coaling", Newport Docks, 1942.

4*

Mynydd Maen ridge

around, too, that sell ropes and ships' tackling, and they smell of the sea), and along the counter-rail of the post-office a talking parrot sidles, and there are birds in cages: all much more reminiscent of Treasure Island than an offshoot of a Government department.

The area near the Docks goes by the old name of Pill-gwenlly, which, with land the other side of the river, is about the only flat land in the town. Pillgwenlly, more familiarly "Pill", or "down Pill", is the name given to a much greater area than is accurate. The old Pill Harriers of Rugby fame were as well known as the Newport team itself.

Of all the sports which take place in Newport, no one, not the most ardent cricketer, or even swimmer (and Newport has turned out some fine swimmers, men and women, of international calibre), can deny that Rugby is *the* game of which Newport, and Monmouthshire as a whole, can always be proud, in the past without doubt, and there is no need to fear for the future. The Valley teams, with their robust play, have always had an enthusiastic following, and have a fame of their own. I am writing this, too, when the Welsh team, captained by John Gwilliam, of Monmouth, who has played for Newport, has made a remarkable recovery and has won the Triple Crown (1950) for the first time for thirty-nine years.

Some sort of Rugby had been played in Newport prior to the eighteen-seventies, but it was not until 1875 that the real game began, and this was at what is now Shaftes-bury Park, where cricket was also played and had more prominence than Rugby. Soon after this, both games moved to the present site of the Newport Athletic Club and the activities of the Club expanded.

After the knickerbocker style, the fashions of the foot-ballers have not altered very much throughout the years, but the various officials who decorate each end of the numerous "groups" provide a complete dress history, from the days of boat-shaped bowlers and long overcoats, through the days when bowlers became more circular, and a sprinkling of large, flat caps gave variety, to the less formal days of no headgear at all. Apart from the change in dress, there is a comforting stability in the Rugby photographs. There are the famous, and those who were just in the team—and what teams some of them must have been.

The first Invincible team to wear the black-and-amber jerseys brought their honours to the game and to their club in the 1891/92 season, and the quality stayed right through until the season of 1896/97. There were 170 matches played, of which 143 were won, 13 lost, and 14 drawn, while in sixteen international matches 98 places were filled by members of the Newport team. I have taken some of these facts from the writings of Mr W. J. Townsend Collins, "Dromio" to all readers of sports news, because he knew the days of the great men of Rugby. The ones I would mention are the ones whose names have been passed down in the history of the game —Harry Packer, Bert Gould, F. H. Dauncey, Percy Phillips, Wallace Watts, C. J. Thomas. Then there were T. C. Graham, Jim Hannan, E. Coulman, Leonard Heard, F. C. Parfitt, T. Pook, George Thomas, T. Newcombe, A. E. Henshaw, T. Down, and H. T. Day, and so many others that it seems wrong to name some while leaving others out; however, these names appeared more often in the team than others.

This was when the greatest three-quarter, Arthur Gould, was playing. He must have been a handsome man, and perhaps the best way of describing his qualities would be to quote the tablet above the memorial bed in the Royal Gwent Hospital at Newport:

> To the memory of Arthur Gould—Greatest of Rugby Football Players—Captain of Newport, Captain of Wales—the mainstay in their Invincible Seasons of Richmond (1886/7), Middlesex (1887/8), Newport (1891/2), and Wales (1892/3)—this Bed is dedicated by Admirers in Five Continents.

In the 1895/96 season another great player, this time a wing three-quarter, came from the captaincy of Cardiff into the Newport team. This was T. W. Pearson; and there was G. Llewellyn Lloyd, a half-back of fine quality, although his build could never have been heavy. This was the season, too, when George Boots first played for Newport, though he did not appear regularly until 1897/98, at the same time as J. Hodges.

Under the captaincy of Llewellyn Lloyd in 1899/1900, the team reached a good level again, and "Beddoe" Thomas came into the team. The next season a famous player, a former Cardiff captain, looked into the team and back out again, for less than a full season, but he should be brought into Newport's picture because he was the greatest centre of his day, Gwyn Nicholls. The next year brought in two Newport stalwarts, C. M. Pritchard and "Sarspa" Thomas, so called for the famous sarsaparilla sold in the family business at the top of Cardiff Road, and in the Valleys.

C. M. Pritchard came to greatness as a forward in the first decade of the century, when T. H. Vile (Newport's High Sheriff in 1945), Reg. Plummer, J. E. C. (Birdie)

Partridge, and Walter Martin were playing. Out at the Tredegar Arms, Bassaleg, Harry Uzzell has a good selection of "caps" to show his customers.

Tommy Vile and Walter Martin partnered one another in some wonderful games, and under the latter's popular captaincy, in 1912, the South African Springboks were beaten. "Dromio" says, "It was Walter Martin who scored the winning try against the Harlequins in 1910 when Newport won by seventeen points to fifteen through Martin's try scored right at the end of the game."

The Club goes on, and the names of the players, and the supporters, live on too. Perhaps the most ardent supporter Newport has ever had was that jovial figure Tommy Vick, in his bowler hat and black-and-amber jersey on his round frame. There was no doubt about it, Tommy Vick loved Rugby players. As well as being a most energetic and vociferous spectator at the matches, he would follow any player or past-player around the town, for the sheer joy of speaking to him.

The comradeship of the Club was proved during the 1914–18 war, when a Newport Athletic Club Platoon of the 8th Battalion of the South Wales Borderers was formed. They had played together, so it was natural enough that they should go to the war together. Among those who did not come back was C. M. Pritchard, fisherman as well as footballer, who carried his fine spirit into France, and died there.

After the war came another fine period for Newport Rugby. From 1919 to 1921 the play was excellent, and 1922/23 was another Invincible year. Neil McPherson, who later played for Scotland, played then, and Ernie Hammett, Jerry Shea, and Reg. Plummer. In 1921 the whole team was composed of internationals.

53

There are the players of the nineteen-thirties, and the forties once the second world war was over, who trained under the watchful eye of the never-to-be-forgotten Chick Mogford; and now the beginning of the new half-century. Whose will be the names to go down in history? It is probably too early to say. Ken Jones, Wales and Newport, and an Olympic sprinter, will be there, and so many others.

But this is just a record of success, and the real success lies in the lasting comradeship and a certain agelessness in its continuation.

The natural rivals of Newport are the blue-and-black jerseyed Cardiff team. The fervour is up to international pitch. I have been to these matches when the Welsh National Anthem is sung, and it is truly moving. Then the whistle blows, the game begins, and anything might happen. A good Cardiff and Newport match is *really* good, but it is also surprising how high-spirited are the friendly rivals on these occasions!

One interesting fact about the Athletic Club, especially when there is a doubt about this "Is Monmouthshire in Wales?" problem, is that in 1897 the Welsh Lawn Tennis Tournament was brought to Newport and has been played at the Newport courts ever since.

Before setting off to the Valleys, leaving Newport with its soft water for washing, its town which is both local and national, and its hybrid accent, it might be a good idea to quote the best-loved of W. H. Davies' "local" poems here. In it he mentions places which are now almost part of Newport, and certainly they are extensions of the town's residential area. William Henry Davies himself was born in 1871 at the Church House Inn, Portland Street, in the Pillgwenlly district of Newport, and many people have read of his life, full of tragedy and joy, in his *Autobiography of a Super Tramp*. He died in 1940. There are six hundred and thirty-six items in his collected poems, apart from his prose works, and many of the verses are descriptive of the countryside; many are of anonymous places, yet were obviously coloured by love for the county of his birth: many include specific references to his boyhood haunts. So many to choose from. All I want to do here is to introduce the reader to a few places, none of them far from Newport, through the eyes of our own poet:

Days That Have Been

Can I forget the sweet days that have been,
    When poetry first began to warm my blood;
When from the hills of Gwent I saw the earth
    Burned into two by Severn's silver flood:

When I would go alone at night to see
    The moonlight, like a big white butterfly,
Dreaming on that old castle near Caerleon,
    While at its side the Usk went softly by:

When I would stare at lovely clouds in Heaven,
    Or watch them when reported by deep streams;
When feeling pressed like thunder, but would not
    Break into that grand music of my dreams?

Can I forget the sweet days that have been,
    The villages so green I have been in;
Llantarnam, Magor, Malpas, and Llanwern,
    Liswery, old Caerleon, and Alteryn?

Can I forget the banks of Malpas Brook,
    Or Ebbw's voice in such a wild delight,
As on he dashed with pebbles in his throat,
    Gurgling towards the sea with all his might?

Ah, when I see a leafy village now,
   I sigh and ask it for Llantarnam's green;
I ask each river where is Ebbw's voice—
   In memory of the sweet days that have been.

The old castle is said to be the one at Newport, and certainly moonlight would be the only setting to make the castle beautiful today. I have seen it when I have come at night into Newport, by train over the river bridge, with the lights reflected in the water, and the dim silhouette of ancient stones having a certain majesty. This part of Newport is not one of its best aspects, or, at least, not until one is halfway across the bridge and looking towards the Docks and its skyline of derricks; and at night the tall flour-mill ablaze with lights, each window doubled by its reflection in the dark river.

Some of the villages must stay in the poem for the time being, until we come to them in their own domain; Llanwern and Magor we already know, for they are part of the moors and may still admit to being "villages so green". There is a different tale to tell of Malpas. Malpas is now a suburb of Newport, and seems to grow and grow. I know people who have fished for trout in Malpas Brook, but that has not been true for some time, though Bettws, which is near enough to Malpas to make no difference, is still rural.

There is not much record of it, but in the twelfth century a Cluniac monastery was founded at Malpas by Winewald de Badon, a cell of some larger community, and possessing only two monks. The Cluniacs were never very popular in Britain owing mainly to their extremely uncertain moral reputation. The Malpas cell suffered the fate of most others of the same order, and apparently left little impression.

56

More post-war building has taken place at Liswerry than anywhere else in Newport, I should imagine. Before the war Liswerry was becoming a large housing site, and building, since the war, has continued until the flat open land is now a continuation of housing estates. Here and there an old house stands out, or, among the new houses, an incongruous farm, once quite isolated.

So much for W. H. Davies' green villages. But what of Allt-yr-yn? Allt-yr-yn, the family stroll, the lovers' lanes, the children's playground. It alters, as it is bound to, being on the fringe of Newport's residential areas, yet nothing really stops the famous "double-view" from the aptly named Ridgeway: the channel is still there, though one looks over the top of temporary houses to see it, and Twyn Barllwm stands over the unspoiled Henllys country on the other side. There might be more noble scenes, yet the sight of the Mynydd Maen range rising from the fertile valley has a gentle beauty hard to equal. In the centre of the picture are the reservoirs at Ynys-y-fro and the big white farm, then there are the woods and the distant mountains to right and left. Perhaps it is the near-ness of the town that adds to the welcoming view. Towards evening the double view takes on new colours—shadowy hills and a memory of the sunset, with the lights coming up all over the town down in the hollow.

Allt-yr-yn, Malpas, Llantarnam, all on the borders of Henllys, that large rural area which seems to spread the length of the Newport side of Mynydd Henllys. There is the old church at Henllys, not far from the foot of Twyn Barllwm, there is Pentre-Bach, the farmhouse, and once the Grange of Llantarnam Abbey, but there is nothing spectacular about Henllys. Most of the farms are small, and the beauty lies in the woods and hedgerows each side of the steep lanes. Allt-yr-yn is just the start of it, and there are not many of Newport's children who have not fished for tadpoles and tiddlers in the disused canal, or have not crossed the fields towards the reservoirs, paddled in Pant-yr-eos Brook, or climbed up to Twyn Barllwm's tump. Pant-yr-eos—the hollow of the nightingale—a beautiful name. Henllys is neglected by visitors to this part of the country, unless they are directed there by kind friends, or become entangled in the lanes by misdirection or accident; yet there are those who know Henllys and become so attached to it that their walks are taken in no other direction. The lanes go uphill and downhill, often with steep banks on either side, and each turning shows Twyn Barllwm a little nearer, a little farther away, but always there. Saxton's map of Monmouthshire, dated 1577, calls the mountain Tumberlow Hill, which is a comfortable name for the rounded contours of a favourite landmark.

"Days that have been", indeed, for some of W. H. Davies' villages, but not all the old beauty has gone.

CHAPTER III

THE VALLEYS

INDUSTRY and the rural life are very closely linked in Gwent, yet most books dealing with the county ignore one or other of these aspects. I have heard it said that most people who do not know the county believe it to be a land of coal tips and terraced mining villages; on the other hand, many strangers' knowledge stops at the Wye Valley: it might spread over into parts of the Usk Valley, yet rarely goes into the really delightful country of the Usk tributaries just before the mountains take the industrial valleys into their dark folds. Often the mountains are beautiful above the coal mines, and, as everywhere else in the county, to generalise is to give a wrong impression.

It will be difficult to keep within the valleys, because so many activities are common to all, yet there are certain characteristics which belong to each one individually, and it will be more orderly for the reader to know—more or less—which way we are going. On the other hand, there are roads which cross from valley to valley, and we might even want to climb a mountain, and from there we will survey whichever side we please.

As we go farther up the valleys the Welsh accent will become more marked. Welsh will be familiar to the speakers, even if it is not their chosen language; perhaps they belong to a Welsh chapel, or their parents spoke Welsh. The turnabout of the words will be following the Welsh pattern: "Morgan have gone down town",

"There's lovely you look", "There's nice it will be to go down Barry for the day". Campbell's Paddle Steamers leave the Pontoon at Newport all through the summer, and they go down the channel to Weston-super-Mare, round the Lightship, up the Avon, and to various other places. The old "Ravenswood" is always likely to be called the "Ravens'ood", with the first syllable well drawn-out. There is a Welsh expression, more translatable *by* expression than meaning. When I was small I knew it as "Ucker vee", and I knew I should not have walked in the mud, bitten my nails, or the hundred and one other things children get up to. I knew later that the words were "ach y fi", and with a shake of the head they mean just that. And what a lot of Monmouthshire fathers are called "Dada".

In Gwent there are many of the Welsh expressions used, and an occasional Welsh word used as a matter of course. Such a mixture of a county. On a Saturday Newport is much more Welsh than during the week, and on a Wednesday, too, when some of the valley towns have early closing, and the farmers and their wives are in town. The valley 'buses are jammed. "Where's my return ticket to", "By there, look". Perhaps it sounds like a paradox, but the valley dwellers are also known as "from the hills".

Everything is so standardised today that there is not so much distinction of dress in various occupations, but until the recent war, at least, and a certain amount of it remains, the miners wore navy blue serge suits, caps, and white mufflers when out on their Saturday jaunts. Outfitting shops had a special line in caps that would be given display on Saturdays, and a roaring trade was done in that commodity.

There is some sort of difference in the people, even from the rest of the county. It is difficult to define, especially individually; perhaps they are harder, but then their lives have been hard. They are often bitter, and with cause. Within the hardness, they will weep at their singing, and from their hardness they will bring forth music to make others weep. They are the race of the ancient Silures, surely, for they are fighters, even though today most of their fighting is done verbally. Talkers they are, too. They might seem difficult to understand until their way of life is understood. It is no use to generalise again. One person will say that the typical man from the hills is the one who will sing at any function where he is joined by one or more compatriots: that they all go mad at football outings, and wear red berets, and make a lot of noise on the way back. Another will say that the typical valley inhabitant is a chapel-going man who frowns on strong drink and sings only in praise of the Lord. Neither picture is completely true, and, as in all communities, there is a good sprinkling of all types, with the ordinary, average, solid citizen to the fore. Especially today, when the isolation-breaking barriers of films, radio, and increased travel give a surface similarity to all but the most remote parts. Of course the valley people sing—they cannot help it; but they do not live in a perpetual choir as so many popular plays and books would suggest.

In some of the Valleys drama would appear to be taking first place in the entertainment and artistic life of the towns and villages, but I will write of that in due course. That might be something to do with education, as singing is often sheer instinct, coupled with the natural Welsh talent and urge in that direction, whereas drama is probably at source a matter of instinct but in development a question of education, and, on the whole, the valley people are gluttons for education. I would not like to state that opinion in type of any great blackness, because the instinct that rises in a Welshman's music is like an ancient culture, stronger than any "education" to be obtained today. And there is an inborn culture in the Welsh, who have retained something of the old bardic tradition and folk-lore.

There were bad times in the Valleys in the early nineteenth century, but not until the years between the two world wars was the widespread degradation of mass unemployment known, the peak being about 1932. The causes of this have been discussed and argued by social workers, politicians, and the unemployed themselves. The story of the mines, from the days of the old ironmasters and colliery owners, until nationalisation on the 1st January, 1947, is a specialised one: with stories of dreadful conditions, strikes, riots, tragic disasters, and gradual improvements, but always the danger. I can only touch on them lightly.

The legacies of bitterness and poverty remain, but the bad times have gone for the time being, with a war to help them on their way, of all ironic happenings. But the fear is always present. The old coal veins will not last for ever, but there are new ones to reach, and there are new methods of mining. Then there are the new industries in the Valleys. Very many young people left South Wales in the nineteen-twenties and thirties. Right away from the Valleys they went, not to Newport or Cardiff, because they too were hit by the depression: they left mainly for the Midlands and for London. Perhaps they never lose that "hiraeth"—a nostalgic longing—which seems inherent in every Welshman.

The Pilgrim Trust, in their report of 1938 of the "special areas", choose the Rhondda as a test-case for South Wales, but an extract from their report would read equally well for the Monmouthshire Valleys: "They are not part of the world outside, but belong to a world of their own. . . . They have a responsiveness to leadership, a strong community spirit, high standards. . . ." It is a thing I had taken for granted before I read the report, but it makes a point that in most other places where unemployment is widespread the general living standard strikes the level of the slum, whereas in the South Wales coalfields the problem is of the middle class, because the general standard is so high and remains so throughout the distress, though food and clothing are scarce, and even hope has gone. Although this is quite true, it does not hide the fact that there are some dreadful conditions of housing in the Valleys. Nevertheless, there has always been a tremendous pride, deep down, that nothing seems to move. It almost seems as though the old unconquerable spirit of the Silures is still there.

The towns come one after the other, built narrowly above the polluted rivers, terraced up the lower slopes of the mountains in most cases, sometimes difficult to know where one town stops and the next one begins. Coal, iron and steel, tinplate, and the subsidiary industries, and now the new lighter industries, give the Valleys their life. There are farms, too, on the mountains, beyond the towns.

The country places have their church; some have a chapel and a church. Likewise in the valley towns, but the various nonconformist denominations predominate. They vie with each other in great number. The square chapel buildings of Penuel, Zion, and the rest look as unrelenting as the hills against which they are built—and from them issues sweet music.

I do not know what the ratio of Italian-owned cafés would be to the native-owned cafés, but I imagine it to be quite high. The fathers and mothers have usually been over here thirty years or more, and their children, as Italian-looking as their parents, speak in the vernacular of the hills. The old hokey-pokey carts, brightly painted, have now become chromium-plated restaurants specialising in coffee, fish and chips, and ice-cream (hokey-pokey by any other name . . .). It is still a well-known sight to see a little covered cart, highly decorative and sparkling with shining paint, being pulled by a trotting pony with bells on its harness, and to see the vendor holding the reins from inside the wagon. It is rather a gay sight, and a jolly sound, when the pony trots along with his red, white, and blue cart, and the bells tinkle. The name written on the cart is invariably Italian.

Carnivals and fêtes are always popular in and around the Valleys; this might be an elementary form of drama, or it might be escapism from dull surroundings. There are little fêtes and big ones, for children and adults. I have been to a purely local affair, like the one in the field near Forge Hammer, above Cwmbran, when the children came dressed in an amazing collection of clothes; and there are the big ones in Pontypool Park which attract enormous crowds and have many kinds of diversion for entertainment and profit. Before the Ministry of Health took control of hospitals the Royal Gwent Hospital was aided by a huge carnival and fête held in Newport during the first week in August of each year.

The fête went on all the week, and on the Thursday

The Western valley
Industrial scene, Ebbw valley

afternoon the streets were full of those gigantic carnival heads, processions of motley mummers, Red Indians and cowboys mounted on all kinds of steeds; a conglomeration of children and adults in every weird costume imaginable, clowns, schoolboys, and men in football jerseys and funny hats, collecting a rain of coppers from every direction; Morris dancers dancing their way along the road; bands and loudspeakers, lorries decorated with beautiful girls. Somewhere in pride of place went the Royal Horse Artillery who were once stationed at the Barracks in Newport, and who wore wonderful uniforms and rode magnificent horses. There was everything. I believe it was one of the finest carnivals in Britain. I know it was always great fun to watch, and then to go on to the fête, which ended with a firework display very late at night.

From the most dignified citizen to the smallest child, not a person went without a carnival mascot worn on his coat for the week. From the Valleys came the character bands. Now these were not brass or silver bands, also a great feature of valley life, but a type of percussion band, and the musical skill was secondary. The main feature was the parade-ground perfection of movement and marching, and the harmony of dress. There was something almost uncanny in the precision of these teams of "Hussars" or "Spaniards", in a conventional notion of costume, and they were also very gay in red, white, and blue, or orange and black. We do not see them in Newport now that the big carnival days are over, but they still compete at different places, including any big events at Pontypool Park, but juveniles have now mostly taken over. In the dark days these bands gave some lightness to life in the mining towns: in one of Idris Davies' poems from his

St Julian's
The Vale of Usk from Wentwood

book *Angry Summer*, the summer of 1926 and the General Strike, he writes:

> Brass bands in all the valleys
> Blaring defiant tunes,
> Crowds, acclaiming carnival,
> Prize pigs and wooden spoons.
>
> Dust on shabby hedgerows
> Behind the colliery wall,
> Dust on rail and girder
> And tram and prop and all.
>
> High summer on the slag heaps
> And on polluted streams,
> And old men in the morning
> Telling the town their dreams.

All this, of course, is modern valley life, and when a South-Walian thinks of the Valleys, his subconscious mind thinks of football, choirs, the Chapel; coal and iron and steel; retired grocers and their nice little bit put away; the general drapers' shops called Paris House, London House, or the Emporium; Temperance Halls and Workmen's Halls, where billiards and a library have often given a glimmer of relief during times of unemployment; silicosis, and the new light industries; a good old talk, and a nice gibbon onion and a bit of cheese for supper. But when I write of each individual river valley, then history will play its part. Often one town could be interchanged for another today, with little difference known, but while industry was new, and before the big works and collieries came, there was a different tale to tell.

THE RIVER RHYMNEY

The curlews of Blaen Rhymni are calling in the night,
And all the hills are magical because the moon is bright,
And I walk alone, and listen, along the mountain way,
To curlew calling curlew in hollows far away.

And the crying of the curlew makes more sad and strange and
    fair
The moon above the moorland and the clear midnight air,
And the mountain breeze is laden with some echoes that must be
The echoes of a music beyond humanity.

And curlew calls to curlew, and I remember as I go
The merrier sounds and echoes out of seasons long ago,
When the nights were full of laughter and all the days were
    bright,
And the heart too young to listen to the curlew in the night.
        Idris Davies: "The Curlews of Blaen Rhymni."

The Rhymney forms the boundary between Glamorgan and Monmouthshire, and flows into the sea near Cardiff. At the mouth of the river Glamorgan holds far more authority than Monmouthshire, and certain land near Llanrumney Hall has, in fact, been handed over to the Glamorgan authorities for use as a housing site. Great trouble this has caused in the council meetings.

Near Llanrumney, at Began, was the fourteenth-century home of the Kemeys, who moved in the fifteenth century to Cefn Mabli, but who, from the Conquest to 1700, had important Gwent connections.

Before the mountains close in there is some really lovely country. This is right on the boundary line, and the woods and hills which make dark beauty of the scenery towards Cefn Mabli and Ruperra, and Coed Cefn Pwll-du, where the Romans had lead mines, are in Glamorgan. All the land looks well tended, with its red earth ploughed and the hedges pruned to an unusual precision. Even where the lanes are grassy down the centre, the hedges each side are neat—there is none of the exuberant profusion of many of the Gwent hedgerows. This is in contrast to the almost wild look of the subdued, distant hills. They lie there quietly enough, yet they have no look of friendliness, especially when the winter trees are black upon their sides. No, not black, for they have blue in them, and a kind of green, or is it purple? They are dark, I know, in the winter, after the blaze of autumn.

Michaelstone-y-Fedw is a village divided into two by a stretch of lane. Down by the bridge is the main group of cottages, the chapel, and the post office, while up on the hill is the school, the church, and the Cefn Mabli Arms. Here again Glamorgan is almost mixed up with Monmouthshire as the river winds. It is difficult to remember that Ruperra is over the border, as it is linked with the Monmouthshire Morgans and the Lower Machen district; and Cefn Mabli is another very near neighbour, and is, in fact, in Michaelstone parish. Michaelstone's original name was Llanvihangel-y-Fedw—another Llan-vihangel or St Michael's—and in this case the Llan-vihangel was turned into Michaelstone: Michaelstone-y-Fedw, or St Michael's by the Birch Tree.

Towards Machen the mountains begin to close in. There is something about this part of the valley—weird, I was going to say, but perhaps that is too definite. The little road beyond the church lies at the bottom of the mountain—Mynydd Machen—but sometimes in the winter the mountain is not there at all. There is just a greyness. I do not mean a decided mist, but almost a grey nothingness. In the summer, of course, Machen Mountain *is* there, whimberries and all, and there is a lot of green in

68

the woods all around. I know someone who saw a fairy on the mountain once. I do not know anything about fairies, but I certainly would not disbelieve this one's existence. The strength of the local brew is not known to me either, but this fairy was seen with sober eyes, I swear.

This is where Castell Meredydd is marked on the map, the castle an ancestor of the Morgans built in the twelfth century. In the winter the trees on the hills of Coed Cefn Pwll-du and Coed Craig Ruperra lie against the grey skyline like black lace. In the Draethen Woods, just over the boundary, are the most wonderful bluebells, and the woods are famous for their primroses. From Rhiwderin to Machen there are narrow lanes at the side of Coed Bedw —the birch wood—and through the woods where the bluebells grow in great profusion. On Machen Mountain, and on most of the hilltops of Gwent, grow the mellow, warm-flavoured whimberries, making the most delicious tarts imaginable. Whimberries are not easy things to pick, growing close to the ground and the berries close to the little stems and leaves, and the juice dyeing one's hands to purple; but what delight they are to eat.

Lower Machen lies between the mountains. All around are the hills, and in the distance the first sign of the coalfields—a conical hill amongst the rounder contours, denoting a coal tip, yet far enough away for the stranger to mining country to wonder how many "sugar loaves" there are.

Plas Machen was one of the early Morgan residences, being built at the end of the fifteenth century by Thomas Morgan, but it has now lost much of its former splendour. In the sixteenth century Leland drew attention to the law of gavelkind when he said: "There is a nother of the

Morgans dwelling by Remny at Maghen, having a fair house. He had bene a man of fair landes, if his father had not devidid it partely to other of his sunnes." The church at Lower Machen bears proof of the family's importance in the district. Around the walls are the painted hatchments of various members of the family. (I understand hatchments were hung on the outside walls of the deceased's house for six months before being removed to the church.) There are many Morgan memorials, including that to Sir William Morgan of Tredegar who died in 1731, aged thirty-one, and who had already achieved fame in politics in the Walpole era, having become the county's Member of Parliament at the early age of twenty-two. His character, though of exceptionally short duration for development, had made an excellent impression, and was exalted in his epitaph in Lower Machen church:

Though he came when young to the possession of
Power, Honour, an high Alliance, and a Great Estate;
Yet they neither made him forget himself
Nor his father's friends;
He was a stranger to Insolence, Oppression, or Ingratitude,
Humane, Courteous and Benevolent
In his Conversation and at Table, Sprightly
Free and Engaging
A lover of his neighbours, Compassionate and Charitable;
Aimiable for these, and other good qualities,
And much lamented at his untimely death.

When we come to the Usk Valley, we will find that his

daughter inherited her father's virtues and even improved upon them.

For forty-two years, from 1831 to 1873, Charles Augustus Samuel Morgan, son of Sir Charles Morgan of Tredegar, held the living of Machen. Two bequests are recorded on the wall of the church, one headed "Benefaction to the Poor", and was made by Hugh Jones "by his Will dated Oct. 1st 1777". He bequeathed £300 to Charles Morgan of Tredegar for the use of the poor of the parish. The other bequest was made by Katherina Morgan of Ruperra in a will dated the 27th June, 1820. This good lady left £250, and when the interest on this was sufficient, land was to be purchased and the rents and profits therefrom were to be spent on "bread and blanketting for ye poor of ye Parish of Machen for ever". And by the same will "20 Shillings per Ann^m to pay for ye Schooling of two poor Boys of ye s^d Parish for ever".

Mynydd Machen and Mynydd Grug, which divide the lower Rhymney Valley from the Sirhowy Valley are, from the Rhymney side, partly wooded and partly bracken covered, with a certain amount of grazing land on the lower slopes. Over the border, on the other side of the river, there is more industry, and there is Caerphilly in the centre of a plain, with the black silhouette of the big castle, like a piece of cut-out scenery, slightly misted with smoke. But in Monmouthshire this part of the valley is more agricultural than industrial, and rather far removed from a first idea of "the Valleys". Mynydd Grug, the mountain of the tump, or mound, is well named, as it has, in fact, several tumuli in the vicinity.

Trethomas and Bedwas are an isolated patch of industry on the Monmouthshire side of the Rhymney before reaching Maes-y-cwmmer. In *Wild Wales* George

Borrow describes a conversation he had with a miner during his tour in this district in 1854:

"The scenery soon became very beautiful—its beauty, however, was to a certain extent marred by a horrid black object, a huge coal work, the chimneys of which were belching forth smoke of the densest description.

'Whom does that work belong to?' said I to a man nearly as black as a chimney sweep.

'Who does it belong to? Why, to Sir Charles.'

'Do you mean Sir Charles Morgan?'

'I don't know. I only know that it belongs to Sir Charles, the kindest hearted and richest man in Wales and in England too.' "

Industry, for all the prosperity it brings, for all its gifts of taken-for-granted comforts, has always been much maligned.

At Bedwas is the Becker Coke Oven Plant erected for British Benzol and Coal Distillation Limited for the manufacture of by-products such as benzol and tar, with its huge storage tanks capable of a working capacity of 20,000 gallons in some cases. The existing plant of the Bedwas Navigation Colliery Company provides the steam and electric power supply for British Benzol.

Trethomas, or Thomastown, as it is sometimes called, adjoins Bedwas. The Valleys are full of place-names derived from personal names, sometimes more remotely, as Tir Shon Jenkins. Trethomas is Welsh enough, but Wattsville and Jamesville in other valleys are not, and neither is Elliott's Town, farther up the Rhmyney. Apart from this kind of pedestrian name the valley towns are often colourfully named, and interesting in their derivation, even though the places themselves are not. Twyn Shon Evan, part of Mynydd Grug, is an unusual name, while Fleur-de-Lis, towards Pengam (part of which is in Monmouthshire, the other part being over the border), is an unexpected name in a Welsh valley, even though it is more than likely to be called "The Flower" by its residents.

Any slow train is affectionately called "The Brecon and Merthyr" in these parts. The present line along the Rhymney is the old Brecon and Merthyr route, and even now the train is out of breath as it puffs up the valley. The conversion of the very old Rhymney tramway took place in 1861, and in 1863 the Brecon and Merthyr Railway Company took over the line, for transporting coal down to Newport and the Docks. Its speed, or lack of it, is legendary.

I suppose the lower Rhymney stands up well against the other valleys as far as scenery is concerned, but I have a feeling that the tree-covered slopes and distant mountains of western Monmouthshire are shunned more for their reputation than anything else. Think of the big industrial cities where a breath of fresh air is an alien thing. Not many valley dwellers have far to go to reach the clear air of the heights, sometimes through the back door and up the hill at the back. I know the rivers are polluted and that coal mines gash the mountains with their industry, yet the worst part of the Valleys is their biased reputation. Once more I would liken places to people: you know the folk who have a reputation for this or that, usually not particularly commendable, and the reputation tends to hang about for a long time. That is sometimes a pity, because to know the person—or place—is to find them quite nice after all. I am not trying to say that the valleys of the coal districts are like the Black Mountains and the Usk Valley, but there is not much wrong with the clear mountain air as it blows over the gorse bushes. Along the Bryn from Maes-y-cwmmer to Pontllanfraith is like that. Then industry breaks in again, and across the valley is a black coal-tip, as tall as the mountains, perhaps taller. One group makes a range of its own, decreasing in size at both sides of the huge main cone.

The northern towns of the Rhymney Valley perhaps compare more accurately with the conventional picture of mining towns. On the Glamorgan and Monmouthshire sides of the river the valley is closed in, the hills are more bare of vegetation, and the blackness of the tips spreads into what was once the green of the mountainsides. The river makes the boundary between the two counties, yet the towns often go in pairs, as though the river makes no boundary at all. There is Pengam, Glam., and Pengam, Mon., then Bargoed and Aberbargoed, the tips of the latter creeping up towards old Bedwellty church and the more open country over the mountain. Tir-phil and New Tredegar would join, but for the narrow, black river; and Pontlottyn and Rhymney are neighbours. Some of the places along the northern reaches of the Rhymney still bear traces of their hard past. The works and collieries seem more condensed in a small space than in the other valleys.

I have seen sheep, mountain ponies, crows, and seagulls all feeding at the same small, bare tip.

Rhymney itself has a wide main street, with stone-built houses and shops along it, and a quiet, old-fashioned air. In the early nineteenth century the Crawshay Bailey connection was developing the iron and coal resources of the valley, and some of the older towns and villages which were built at that time still belong very much to that period. Much of the industry of this part of the valley went through the hands of Richard Crawshay to Benjamin Hall, and this property included the old Union Iron Works.

THE SIRHOWY VALLEY

"Many are the attempts made to arrive at the proper derivation of the word Sirhowy, but the most appropriate is the one offered by Eiddil Gwent, viz., *Sir* being the root of the word *Siriol* (pleasant and cheerful), and *gwy* or *wy* being the old Welsh word for water, hence the meaning of the word, according to the above etymological definition, is *Pleasant* or *Cheerful Water*."—Evan Powell, from *The History of Tredegar*, 1884.

Not far from Risca, but nearer to Cross Keys, the Sirhowy runs into the Ebbw. "Then Ebwith, and with her slides Srowy", said the seventeenth-century spelling of Michael Drayton.

When the Reverend Coxe visited Monmouthshire in 1798 the land had not been changed by the growing industrial encroachment (and he did not venture far north):

"Having breakfasted", he wrote, "we mounted our horses, rode along the vale, and crossed the Ebwy near the influx of the Sorwy, over Pont y Cymmer; where I observed recent traces of the terrible ravages occasioned by the inundation of the torrent. Soon afterwards we ascended the side of the hill, which bounds the vale, and continued along an elevated ridge, through thickets, corn fields, and meadows, sprinkled with hamlets, watered by numerous torrents, and overlooking the Sorwy. The features of this vale are more wild and romantic than those of the Ebwy; it is narrower and

75

deeper; and the shelving declivities, laid out in meadows, stretch to the edge of the torrent, which roars in a profound abyss, obscured by overhanging trees."

The steep slopes of Mynydd Grug, cut by short, rushing streams, close in on the one side, and the slightly less forbidding Mynyddislwyn rises on the other side. While all around the mountains are the collieries, Mynyddislwyn has its fair share of agriculture, and leaning on a gate at one of the highest points I have seen how the mountains rise from the valleys; and overhead the curlews cried.

It still surprises me to see Mynyddislwyn church set on the mountainside, alongside Twyn Tudur (Tudur was a Welsh saint, but the tumulus must date back to much more ancient days), though one old account—there are several versions—indicates that it should have been built at a much higher position, possibly high on Mynydd y Lan. The priests in charge of the building were not happy at the thought of the work involved in hauling the stone up the mountainside to the very top, so each night a white-clad horseman on a white horse carried a certain amount of the building material taken there during the day farther down the hillside, calling to the night sky, "I'r llwyn! I'r llwyn!" ("To the grove! To the grove!"), and this was taken to be a sign that the church should be built where the white figure deposited the material each night. So much for superstition: it had its uses in the past.

Soon after the long severity of the winter of 1947 I was talking to someone living at Mynyddislwyn, and she told me how her young son went to fetch the milk from the farm. Normally it was a round-about way, but during the snows he could take a short cut over the top of the hedges of two lanes to reach the farm by a direct route. This went on until the thaw set in, for if he had gone then he could have dropped through the snow and been completely covered.

> Oh! mighty overshadowing Tree!
> Where is the hand that planted thee?
>> The plant lives on,
>> The planter gone!

> Oh! mighty castle by the sea!
> Where is the hand that builded thee?
>> The building stands,
>> The plant lives on,
>> The builder and the planter gone!

Those are the first two verses of a poem by Islwyn, the bardic name of William Thomas, who was born in 1832 near Ynysddu, and who took his bardic title from the district he loved. His mother was from Newbridge, though his father came from farther afield, Ystradgynlais. Young William Thomas, after his education in Glamorgan, Tredegar, and Newport, should have become a mining engineer, but his heart called him to religion, and he became a Calvinistic Methodist minister. Most of his verse was in Welsh, though he wrote a certain number of poems in English. His sympathies were always with Wales, and once he refused a more prosperous living in England to stay with his own people. In looks he was of the small and slender type of Welshman, with dark colouring, and his writings are full of the sombre longing of his race.

Most of the great preachers have had a command of "hwyl", that stirring eloquence rising to an emotional cry of praise, but Islwyn's voice was soft and gentle, yet he was a great preacher as well as a poet, and beloved by his congregation. He was only forty-six when he died in 1878, but his name is perpetuated in the Mynyddislwyn area of the Sirhowy Valley.

For all the industry that now almost surrounds them, two Tudor houses, both farms today, remain in something of their old beauty. Penllwyn Fawr and Plas Bedwellty were both homes of the Morgans. Edmund Morgan of Bedwellty was the fourth son of Thomas of Machen, and it was his eldest son who lived at Penllwyn, and the family lived there until the middle of the eighteenth century, when the line died out with Henry Morgan, a most popular man in the district.

This collateral branch of the Morgans served their county as Sheriffs, Henry of Penllwyn in 1588, Rowland of Bedwellty in 1593, Henry of Penllwyn in 1603. Then there was a long break until 1700, when Edmund of Penllwyn was Sheriff. In 1722 and 1734 another Henry Morgan took office. It was a sign of the approach of industry in the nineteenth century that one of the famous ironmasters, Samuel Homfray of Bedwellty, became Sheriff in 1841. He was not a Monmouthshire man, but married a sister of Sir Charles Morgan. Bedwellty in this case is not the old Plas Bedwellty, but is farther up the valley, at Tredegar.

Bedwellty House was built at the height of the industrial prosperity, and the park and house now belong to the town of Tredegar. It is noticeable that Members of Parliament and Sheriffs were tending in the nineteenth century to be the ironmasters and colliery owners, although the old family names are still there, but the industrial growth is very evident.

Bedwellty also gives its name to one of the most famous Monmouthshire shows, which is now held at the Showfield, above Blackwood, and until recently was the biggest one-day show in the county. This agricultural show originated in the Tredegar Company's stables in 1880, mainly for the showing of pit-ponies, but it has expanded to include all the usual attributes of agricultural shows. The show is still held on a Monday, the first Monday in each month having been, in the past, a traditional miners' holiday.

Across the hill, through the Showfield at Blackwood, and beyond Maes Rhyddid, is Bedwellty church, looking down into the Rhymney Valley, where the growing coaltips of Aberbargoed rise to the church wall. Across to the other side, the Sirhowy Valley at that particular part makes it difficult to tell that this is industrial Gwent, because the fields are chequered on the hillsides, and in late summer the corn glows golden in the sun. The valley is not crowded beneath the hills, but opens out to a certain extent and is rather more rolling. From the hill above Blackwood town Mynyddislwyn church shows against its hillside squarely, and it might almost be on a rural slope, amidst its fields; but beneath the hills, in the darkness of the earth, are the coal mines.

It is the mines beneath Bedwellty church which have caused the gravestones to sink and crack and the old vaults to open up, but the ancient church itself has withstood well the winds of the hilltops and the tunnelling below. One of the older remaining inscriptions is that written on an iron "tombstone" on the path to the porch, and one which dates back to the early days of the ironworks. It is dated 1778, and shows little signs of the wear which would by now have obliterated a stone placed in a similar exposed position. The remains are those of a gentleman from "the Village of Merthyr Tidvil", which not long afterwards extended the roaring furnaces of the Cyfarthfa Works to make Merthyr more than a village.

This church, dedicated to St Sannan, dates in part to 1220, and has a most unusual vestment chest of great age. On one panel is carved a heart with pierced hands above and pierced feet below, and these symbols of the Crucifixion are surrounded by a crown of thorns.

It is in the Sirhowy Valley that drama flourishes. All over the county there is a new interest in drama, but perhaps it is in Oakdale, Tredegar, and Blackwood that drama is most alive. Several valley societies have been accused of "pot-hunting", and it is true that they go far afield to enter for drama festivals, but their plays have an earnestness unusual in amateur performances. In any case, this is not much more than a continuation of the Eisteddfod spirit. I remember a performance by one society when I felt that the fourth wall was at the back of the Welfare Hall, closing the audience in with the players; not that the audience was on the outside looking in.

Many valley towns hold three-act play festivals for a week at a time—quite an ambition to fill a hall each night for a week with a different play played by a different society. Companies from England and Wales come to Monmouthshire for these events; any night of the festival week there is a play of quality on stage. Newbridge in the next valley is another festival town, and prospective audiences queue the night before for tickets. And if this sounds too much like the Old Vic or Covent Garden, then it must not be forgotten that the professional theatre is sadly lacking in Monmouthshire. What is done has to be done by the people themselves.

The Square, Caerleon-on-Usk
Roman Amphitheatre, Caerleon-on-Usk

THE VALLEYS

Only when plays sponsored by the Arts Council arrive at the various halls do the Valleys (and even Newport, if it comes to that) see professionally acted plays. There is a real welcome when the players have their "one night stands" at the Welfare Hall, Tavarnaubach, right up in the hills on the northern fringe of the coalfields. The Workmen's Halls at Blaenavon, Llanhilleth, and Tredegar (and Tredegar attracts fine artists in the musical world) are a little nearer to populous parts, but no nearer to a theatre than Tavarnaubach, so they welcome the Western Theatre Company Players too, and at the Workmen's Institute at Pengam. Unfortunately, this great event is also a rare one, but the numerous local societies make up the deficiency with their own natural talents.

The Monmouthshire Drama League was founded in 1931, when a small meeting took place at the Three Salmons, Usk, and now there are more than one hundred and fifty affiliated societies, and there must be a like number of smaller societies operating all over the county.

Industry was growing in this valley some time in the early nineteenth century, and in 1802 the Sirhowy Valley Tramway Act was passed for the building of a railroad from Nine Mile Point Colliery to Newport, and later this was extended to the Sirhowy Works near the head of the valley. These old railroads (or tramways) were the originators of the present-day railways, coming from pack-mule trails, horse-drawn trams owned by the industrial companies, early steam-engines in the name of small railway companies, and finally being amalgamated with the Great Western Railway Company and into the anonymity of British Railways.

Some of the old collieries are derelict, and their tips are growing green again, but others, like the Wyllie

6*

81

Twyn Square, Usk
Rood Screen, Llangwm

Colliery, are heaping their tips freshly towards the mountain tops. Oakdale is in the nature of being a model town and colliery, and brings modern planning to an old industry.

The mountains towards Tredegar are less stark than the corresponding mountainsides of the Rhymney Valley. There is an incongruous mixture of farms and trees on the hilltops and coal-tips low in the river valley. In the autumn the golden bracken glows against the green of the mountains, and trees break the line of the endless mountain ranges. The land looks less barren than the grey-green of the Rhymney Valley, and cattle as well as sheep crop the grass.

The iron and coal industry was originated in Tredegar about one hundred and fifty years ago, the iron forges, as usual, being first of all powered by charcoal until the potentialities of coal were realised. The Fothergills and Jeremiah and Samuel Homfray were pioneers in the early days, with the Tredegar Iron and Coal Company taking over at a later date. It was the Homfrays, too, who built the first furnace at Sirhowy. By 1864 the Tredegar Iron and Coal Company owned collieries and ironworks at Ebbw Vale, Sirhowy, Abersychan, and Abercarn, apart from various other undertakings throughout the county.

Life in a town such as Tredegar must have been very hard, when women as well as men were employed in the mines, and the conditions of work such as they were, with explosions and disease adding to the misery. Several epidemics of cholera broke out in the eighteen-thirties and forties and even later, and later in the century several explosions occurred in Bedwellty Pit and also Pochin Colliery, among others. The fortune of all the Valleys seemed to be a thing of fluctuation right from the beginning, with periods of prosperity and poverty alternating.

Pack-horses and mules brought the iron and coal to Newport, until, in 1812, a tramroad for horse-drawn trams was opened as an extension from Nine Mile Point. Later the same tramroad was converted into the steam railway.

As the manufacture of steel became increasingly efficient, and when foreign coal competed on the market with Welsh coal, Tredegar faced great difficulties, and by the eighteen-seventies or eighties the old ironworks were almost at a standstill. One of the early Whitehead ventures began at Tredegar in 1903, and in 1914 the company was able to acquire land at Newport.

Like so many of the early iron towns Tredegar, basically, retains many of its old buildings in the main streets, though the façades have a modern look. There is one old shop with a flagstone floor and a low ceiling, which does not look as though it has altered for very many years. Otherwise, apart from this old foundation, Tredegar is a busy place, dominated by its amazing town clock in the Circle. I have never seen such a clock: I doubt if anyone has. The clock is on top of a tall pillar, and underneath that is a great iron base, dated 1858, and made by Jordans, the old Newport ironfounders. The base tells of the bazaar held to pay for the clock, and of the nation's hero, Wellington, but above all is its colour. It is red—a wonderful, bold red. No one could forget Tredegar if they had once seen its clock.

On the road into Tredegar, as on many other roads, is a notice "Beware of Engines". On the mountain road to Rhymney, over Cefngoleu, is a notice "Beware of Sheep", which just shows how life is mingled in the valleys.

A great block of mountains lies across the top of the Monmouthshire valleys, and as the valleys go up into these mountains so the air becomes colder and the land more barren. At the head of each valley is a town of some size or importance—Rhymney on its own river, Tredegar (with Dukestown and Sirhowy) on the Sirhowy, Ebbw Vale (and Beaufort adjoining) on the Ebbw Fawr, and Nantyglo and Blaina on the Ebbw Fach (though Brynmawr on the boundary, and really in Brecknock, is the town at the head of the river). Beyond these towns Mynydd Llangynidr and Mynydd Llangattwg form a natural boundary to the county.

At one point the Monmouthshire boundary shoots up into Mynydd Llangynidr, into the bare mountains, and there the bleak village of Trefil straggles along the mountain, and blasts its living from the stone quarries. There is not much pasture for the sheep, cattle, and mountain ponies that crop the grass between the bracken, and the trees are stunted and windswept. Nant Trefil and numerous swift-flowing streams break over their stony beds on the hillsides, and in places there is even a certain beauty in the landscape. At the bottom of the road to Trefil is the Mountain Air Tavern, most suitably named, as the wind blows over these mountains. Near Tredegar is a Blast Furnace Inn, and up at Trefil a Quarrymen's Arms, so there is no need to wonder what the main industries are, or have been, in these places.

Only mountain tracks go on beyond Trefil, yet I would prefer its isolation to the bleakness of Nantybwch, a new suburb, I suppose you would call it, of Dukestown. Most valley towns have stood up to time and the weather with increasing steadfastness, but Nantybwch looks rather uncared-for now, so I do not know how it will look in the

years to come. But this must be a hard country to live in.
The quarries give forth their stone, and the ground itself
is stony. The bare mountains stretch for miles of empty
isolation, the little streams and rivulets run down into the
roads, and the wind sweeps the treeless ground. At the
height of Trefil one misses the grandeur of mountain
scenery, for one is so high that it is like looking at undulating moorland, as this is near the top of the mountains.
From the high railway line along the top of the Gwent
Valleys the distance of the mountains can be seen, and
something of their pattern.

THE VALLEYS OF THE EBBW

Where Ebbw gurgles to the Usk
  Beauty once reigned in garments green,
Now slag heaps drear and sprawling streets,
  The price of wealth, defile the scene.

Here men, who wrest from earth's dark vaults
  The energy of age-long sun,
That ministers to common weal,
  A pittance gain for riches won. . . .

Shall I forget these dauntless men—
  Despoiled of just inheritance—
Whose toilsome tasks in peril deep
  The comforts of my life enhance?

S. G. Watts (1871–1947), from "Shall I forget?"

The Ebbw joins the Usk near Newport Docks, and
part of it flows through the Wentllwg Level. There are
roads of orange-tiled houses before the bridge goes over
the Ebbw at Tredegar Park, and this is Maesglas. (In our
Newport way this is invariably known as "Maysglas"
instead of "*Myes*glas".) On the other side of the road the

ancient Tredegar Fort looks down on this modern intrusion. In the sixteenth century the poet-chronicler Thomas Churchyard wrote of Greenfield (Maesglas), part of the Duchy of Lancaster:

A fine sweete soyle, most pleasant unto sight,
That for delight, and wholesome ayre so pure. . . .
The pastures greene, the woods, the water cleere, ·
Sayth any prince may buyld a pallace heere.

But before the Ebbw (known variously in the past as Ebwith, Ebwy, Ebboth, Elboth) reaches the outskirts of the town it flows through Bassaleg, and it might have been here that W. H. Davies heard Ebbw's voice "in such wild delight". There is always life in the black, polluted Ebbw as it dashes over the stones at Ebbw Bridge or at Bassaleg, so much life that the two main roads over these bridges are frequently flooded.

Bassaleg church originated when a Benedictine priory was founded by Robert de Haia in 1102. The priory estates, together with those of Machen and Bedwas and several others, were given to the Abbey of Glastonbury, though eventually they came under the jurisdiction of the See of Llandaff. There are Morgan tombs in practically every church of old Wentllwg, and Bassaleg has memorials to many of the Morgans of Tredegar, particularly to those who have died during the last and present centuries.

Through Tredegar Park the Ebbw flows, until it goes under the Cardiff road on to the marshes. Tredegar Park is part of the Tredegar estate given to the public. It stretches from Cardiff road to Bassaleg, part of it used as a golf course, and in a fairly natural condition, overlooked

by the great Iron Age camp, and part of it used as playing
fields and children's play park. The Ebbw flows swiftly
at the side of this park, beneath the railway embankment
which hints at industry farther up the valley. This stretch
of single-line railway is usually known as the Golden Mile,
or, more officially, the Park Mile, for a certain toll was
paid to the Morgans of Tredegar for each truck of coal
transported along this route. Coal from the hills. The hills
you can see in the distance beyond Bassaleg. The railway
was constructed from Nine Mile Point Colliery to the
Canal at Newport, and Sir Charles Morgan was obliged,
while receiving tolls for the trucks using the line, to make
and maintain this particular portion of the railway.

Angharad, the mother of the first Morgan of Tredegar,
had other sons besides Morgan, and one was Ifor, who did
not go far from the fold to set up his own residence. He
lived at Gwern-y-Cleppa, and the meagre remains of this
house are to be found in Gwern-y-Cleppa Wood, which
lies between the main Cardiff road and the Pen-y-lan
road from Bassaleg. The house has probably been in ruins
for a couple of hundred years or more, but in its time it was
a great house, with a benevolent lord, Ifor Hael, Ifor the
Generous.

Ifor Hael was the patron and kinsman of Dafydd ap
Gwilym, a Welsh lyric poet, and supposedly a great lover,
of handsome appearance. Dafydd's poems are, in translation (and they are said to lose much of their beauty in
translation), easy to read and understand, full of the joys
of nature, and of love, too. The precise dates of his birth
and death are not known; one record gives his life from
1325 to 1385, while another, more vague, says he lived
somewhere between 1330 and 1400. Sir H. Idris Bell and
David Bell, who have translated many of the poems, say

he was born between 1320 and 1330, and died between 1370 and 1388. This is the beginning of Sir Idris Bell's translation of "The Poet Makes a House in the Birch Wood":

A happy place is the birch grove
Where of a summer's day I love
To roam paths suddenly seen
Through leafy veils of radiant green;
A close retreat for my gold-clad love,
Where the thrush lords it in the boughs above,
And the green tree answers the green hill-side,
And sweet lovers can safely hide;
For a curtain there screens loved and lover
In the green glade the green leaves cover;
And there will my love and my lady come
To the house God builded to be our home.

The fame of Dafydd has outshone that of his patron, Ifor Hael, who, with his wife, Nest, died of the plague.

The nicest way of getting to Gwern-y-Cleppa Wood (or "Clappa" as it is known locally) is from Cardiff road, walking through the wide avenue of chestnuts that goes up the hill, then through a plantation of pine trees. The wood turns then into a mixed wood, spreading each side, and numerous springs flow, meeting in a hollow that takes a lot of beating for a woodland scene.

At the top of the hill is an Iron Age fort, Graig-y-Saeson, or Coed y Defaid, Saeson indicating Saxon or foreigner, Coed y Defaid being of more modern designation, "wood of the sheep". There are trees on the mound, but through the thin trunks of the larch trees the formation of the fort is easily seen. From here there is a new vision of the mountains. Familiar Twyn Barllwm takes on an altogether larger appearance, and some idea of the ranges can be seen, right around from the Glamorgan mountains to the mountains of northern Gwent.

Farther up the valley, against the flow of the river, Rogerstone is on the other side of the Ebbw, and Rogerstone has grown within recent years from a village to a place of industry, with its great aluminium works. The foundations of Rogerstone are old enough, with its old name of Tre gwillym (still used) from William de Berkerolles, who inherited Bassaleg and adjoining land. Rogerstone comes from the name of de Berkerolles' son, Roger, or even from his father-in-law, Roger de Haia, whose father was the founder of Bassaleg Priory. Every other building in Rogerstone seems to be a chapel of one nonconformist belief or another, or one of the newer religions has its wooden and corrugated headquarters there.

Towards Risca the hills begin to close in, and the three methods of transport run parallel along the valley. There is the river, then the main road, then the Monmouthshire and Brecon Canal, disused now, and very pretty. At one time the coal barges plied the Canal, and here and there, though disappearing quickly now, are a few barges, half-submerged, with weeds growing through the cracks in the timber. On one side of the Canal is the Henllys country, and then the barrier of the Mynydd Maen range.

The Canal is over a hundred and fifty years old, and when it was first built, William Phillips, who lived at Risca House, laid a wager that he would jump his horse over a lock. The horse fell into the lock, and Squire Phillips fractured his skull, but coming from an apparently tough race he survived, with a plate in his head for the rest of his life. William was a grandson of Charles Phillips of Marshfield, and his father had married Amy Walters, who inherited the Tudor dwelling, Risca House. Families were rarely small in those days, and the squire kept well in the fashion with his twenty-six children. Quite a character of the Risca neighbourhood was William, keeping a pack of hounds, and often running them over Mynydd Maen and back on a Sunday just for the fun of it. He presented six pairs of hounds to George III, and the Llangibby Hunt had part of the pack from John Lawrence, who had a pack of his own originated by the Risca hounds.

The Risca hounds hunted very frequently, and were, I believe, the first hounds in the district to be bred exclusively for fox-hunting. Henllys must have been alive with the huntsman calling the hounds with his horn from the cottages where they were kept, and then the noisy cries of the hounds; they were a pack always hunting in full cry, and rarely mute.

Incidentally, people from Risca are known as Risca Cuckoos, for shutting the gate to a field and wondering why the bird has flown.

In 1865 William Brace was born at Risca, and in due course went to work at the Abercarn Colliery until, in 1890, he was elected Miners' Agent. In 1906 Mr Brace was elected Labour Member of Parliament for South Glamorgan, and in nine years' time was appointed Under Secretary of State. He lived his last years of retirement in Newport, and when I was a schoolgirl I can remember on Sunday mornings, as we went for a short walk over Ridgeway, my father would pass the time of the day with an elderly gentleman, walking with great dignity, and afterwards he would say to me, "That was the Right

Honourable William Brace". I was never sure, then, who
William Brace was, or what he had been, but he always
impressed me as being someone of authority: his large
moustache might have added to that impression. I believe
he was known for his sane outlook, and lack of aggressive
rudeness which has coloured the career of some other
politicians.

The mountains above Abercarn are well covered with
forestry plantations, and they make a great dark green
patch against the lighter green of the rest of the mountains. The paths cut through the woods look impossibly
steep, but the wood is being felled and new trees set with
good thought for the future. Some of the timber is used
locally in the pits. Much of the land around Abercarn
belongs to the Llanover and Llanarth estates. This began
when in 1808 Richard Crawshay of the Cyfarthfa Works
at Merthyr bought the Abercarn estate and gave it to his
son-in-law, Benjamin Hall, of Llanover.

Beneath the mountains of Abercarn a tragic mining
disaster occurred at the Prince of Wales pit, in September
1878, when 268 miners lost their lives, some being as
young as thirteen years of age. Such was the local aspect
of a tragedy of this kind that the Primitive Methodist
Chapel lost half its members and the choir was reduced to
one. Religion must have been as ruthlessly deep-rooted
as the elements when the survivors sang to God in the
hour of despair. Probably the conception of religion in the
chapels of the mining valleys, where tragedy is always
waiting to strike, is truer than the softer, conventional
idea, or tragedy would have crushed any superficial
worship. Unless there is a disaster of any size, the outside
world does not hear of the deaths in the pits. It is no uncommon thing in the local paper to read of a miner crushed

91

by a tram or killed by a fall of coal. At the time of the big Abercarn disaster a contemporary poet wrote:

Roll on, thou death-black Ebbw, roll
Thy quiv'ring waters to the sea,
Let a dirge for each departed soul,
Amidst thy murmurs mingled be.

At Crumlin is the great viaduct across from one mountain top to the other, astride the river and dwarfing the works and houses beneath. It is about 200 feet high, and 1,500 feet long, or, with the masonry at each end, about 1,658 feet long. The firm of Kennard Brothers was responsible for its erection, one of the family designing it, and, in fact, the Kennards built most of Crumlin itself. The work was commenced in 1853, and on 1st June, 1857, the viaduct was opened. The iron in its construction was from Garnddyrys, the other side of Blaenavon. In the nineteen-twenties the Crumlin Valley Collieries and various tinplate and steel undertakings were taken over by Partridge, Jones and John Paton Limited, and two more pits were sunk at Crumlin, while in 1937 the Tirpentwys "Black Vein" Steam Coal and Coke Company became part of the great organisation which had connections throughout the county.

At Aberbeeg, known as much for its connection with brewing as anything else, the Ebbw divides into Ebbw Fawr and Ebbw Fach. Aber is confluence, and the "beeg" part of the name comes from the Bîg stream, flowing down the mountain, which is rather odd, when the main confluence here is of the two branches of the Ebbw.

Ebbw Fawr flows through Ebbw Vale, and its name-town houses the great works of Richard Thomas and Baldwins, an undertaking not more than fourteen years

old. Industry developed at Ebbw Vale by the end of the
eighteenth century, and the town originated in 1790.
The rails for the famous Stockton to Darlington railway
were rolled at Ebbw Vale, so progress must have been
quite swift. The people most concerned with the early
growth of Ebbw Vale were Walter Watkins and Jeremiah
Homfray, who, with his brother Samuel, was connected
with much of the industry of Monmouthshire. Ebbw
Vale was one of the first places to use the Bessemer process
in 1856, followed by Rhymney and Blaenavon.

The old Ebbw Vale Company was compelled to close
down its works during the 1920–30 depression, but in
1936 the works were taken over and tremendously enlarged by Richard Thomas and Baldwins, which gave new
life to Ebbw Vale. The town retains enough of its "valley
life" to have an occasional sheep straying into the main
street, which is rather more drab than many of the other
valley towns. The Member of Parliament for Ebbw Vale
is that fiery Aneurin Bevan from Tredegar.

Ebbw Vale is one of the places where Glamorgan play
a county cricket match each year, which, if this does
not sound like a happening in the industrial valleys,
just shows that no generalisation can be made about
them.

Like the rest of the valleys, stories of the supernatural
are manifold in the Ebbw Valleys, and "the old prophet
of Tranch", Edmund Jones, a minister who wrote many
religious works, gave several examples in *A Geographical,
Historical, and Religious Account of the Parish of Aberystruth in the County of Monmouth* (the old parish of Aberystruth is in the Ebbw Fawr valley). This book was
published in 1779, at the price of 1*s*. 6*d*., and at a sale in
1902 a copy was sold for £65. Edmund Jones died in

1793, over ninety-one years of age, and was buried at Ebenezer Chapel, Pontnewynydd.

One man who was well known to Edmund Jones was enticed to the mountains by the music of the fairy-folk, and he was there for a year, dancing, and when he returned to his home again he "looked very bad". If Edmund Jones had never seen or heard a "pwca" himself, then he knew something of their ways, and when they *were* to be seen and heard.

"In the night more than in the day, in the morning and evening of the day more than about noon. Abundance of people saw them, and heard their musick, which everyone said was low and pleasant, but none could ever learn the Tune: Heard their talking like that of many talking together, but the words seldom heard."

Just above Abertillery is Blaenau Gwent—the end of Gwent—but though it might seem the end of the world to some, it is a peculiar place to have Blaenau Gwent. In fact, Blaenau has another meaning. One very early nineteenth-century Welsh dictionary says specifically: ". . . also where valleys terminate or are interrupted by mountains as Blaenau Gwent in Monmouthshire". Ebbw Fach—not much different in size to Ebbw Fawr—flows through Abertillery (at the confluence of the little Tillery stream), the next town in size in the county to Newport. The town seems to me to be built not so much in the valley as in a hole in the mountains, and to get out of it one must climb the sides. The streets are all on sharp hills, and the town climbs the hillsides. Right the way down this valley the mountains are close and steep: there is a formidable ridge all the way from Nantyglo.

Abertillery was developed rather later than many of the colliery towns, the railway to Newport being built in 1845. In 1850 the South Wales Colliery Company began its activities in the district, and soon the whole area was under production.

Nantyglo and Blaina were being developed in the early days of industrial growth. These two towns were, and are still, connected, and with them went Beaufort, although it is nearer Ebbw Vale. It was grouped with Nantyglo and Blaina as part of the Crawshay Bailey territory. The Nantyglo Iron Works were opened in 1789 and purchased by Crawshay Bailey in 1813, the family firm retaining its interest until 1870. In the early part of its tenure there were seven blast furnaces at Nantyglo and five at Beaufort, together with the usual forges and rolling mills.

The name of Crawshay Bailey has always been connected with one of the most colourful figures of the industrial era. He was the nephew of Richard Crawshay who came from Yorkshire and leased the Cyfarthfa Works at Merthyr in 1786. In 1794 he bought them, and his wealth increased. Crawshay Bailey went to Merthyr as a poor little boy, and worked his way to being one of the chief industrialists in Monmouthshire, building railways, sinking pits, and putting forward plans for canals, all because he realised the great future in coal. He was for many years Member of Parliament for Monmouthshire and Newport Boroughs.

But whatever else Crawshay Bailey did, and he was a man of independent character, he and his railway schemes will always go together. There is a song—the verses vary (unprintable and otherwise)—all about Crawshay Bailey and his engine. It is one of those songs which go on and on for ever, according to the memory of the singer, and it is always sung with a good old Welsh accent:

> Crawshay Bailey had an engine,
> And he found it wouldn't go,
> So he pulled it by a string,
> All the way to Nantyglo.
> Chorus: Did you ever see,
> Did you ever see,
> Did you ever see
> Such a funny thing before?
>
> Crawshay Bailey had an engine,
> She was puffin' and a-steamin',
> And accordin' to her power
> She could do four miles an hour.
> Chorus: Did you ever see, etc.

But for all that, Crawshay Bailey did get the railways and canals built to take his precious coal down to Newport.

Nantyglo and Blaina still have an old-world look about them, with a Victorian neatness in the stone cottages and Blaina's main street with its small shops.

The Ebbw Valleys are steep and close, valleys which have seen hard times within their narrow confines. Yet the impression of the whole is of an indomitable pride.

THE AFON LLWYD

> A tree wild with wind
> Like a billowing ship,
> And scavenging sheep
> On a black coal-tip;
> A silhouette of pit-wheels
> That spin overhead,
> Like spiders caught close
> In their own cunning thread.
>
> Myfanwy Haycock, from "Return".

Afon Llwyd—grey water—a good name today for the

Raglan Castle

polluted river which is a tributary of the Usk, joining its
parent at Caerleon. Grey might suggest a slow, sluggish
river, but the Afon Llwyd is full of high spirits, a *black*,
bounding river. Michael Drayton, in 1622, found it one
of the more pleasant tributaries of the Usk:

When Avon cometh in, than which amongst them all
A finer is not found betwixt her head and fall.

Although the Afon Llwyd has its rural moments, its
main journey is through industrial Blaenavon, Abersychan, and Pontypool. Cwm Afon is a valley of industry.

Before Cwmbran, where industry begins in earnest, is
Llantarnam. For Llantarnam I have a particularly soft
spot, although there is now a biscuit factory placed
discreetly in a hollow adjoining the railway station. Llantarnam is one of my old familiar places, and the memories
come crowding in, of village cricket, garden fêtes, six-
pennyworth of ice-cream filling a vegetable dish,
numerous minor accidents, and all the country joys and
tribulations of childhood. The village is another of the
half-and-half places near the big towns. The old remains,
but the new is pushing and pushing, nearer and nearer.

The village has a square, castellated church tower, next
to the Greenhouse, a country pub of pleasant exterior
appearance, and both are hung about with trees, while
opposite the church is a smithy. Over the porch of the inn
is an unusual sign. What a pity it is that not more of our
inns have good signs outside. The Cefn Mabli Arms at
Michaelstone-y-Fedw should have the Kemeys heraldry
outside, for the Kemeys lived at Cefn Mabli at one time. At
Llanvihangel-nigh-Usk there is the little Herbert Arms,
and that has a colourful coat of arms at the cross-roads.

Abergavenny

The sign at the Greenhouse is quite unusual, and is set in the round gable of the porch. Two jolly little men are carved (and coloured), sitting at a table set with an outsize goblet, a candle, and a jug, the jug being almost as big as the men. Their coat tails drop over the chairs as they sit there, while one fellow has a pipe or horn in his mouth. Underneath the picture are the Welsh words:

Y Tu Gwyrdd
1719
Cwrw da
A Seidir i chwi,
Dewch y mewn
Chwi gewchy brofi

which mean:

The Green House,
1719
Good ale and cider for you
Come in: you shall taste it.

The Abbey is hidden from view, but if you go through the churchyard you come to the Abbey parkland. Within recent years the aspect of the grounds has altered, because the estate was sold during the past few years and the land split up and sold to various local farmers. The parkland is fenced through the centre, the big trees are being felled, and the cultivation of crops is taking place. Two streams, the largest being the Dowlais Brook, polluted with waste from the ironworks, and brick red in colour, flow sluggishly through the park, but once over the second wooden bridge very little change can take place. The ground is undulating and bracken-covered, with a clear stream running in the hollow, and the trees are a joy in any season: there is a giant beech, and its roots have made a deep hollow filled with its own golden leaves. Then there is a white-blossomed cherry-tree, a spring fairy-tale among its more sedate neighbours. The bushes are the haunts of birds, and I have watched red squirrels leaping from branch to branch with complete grace.

It is fitting that the cross-roads and the inn near the Magna Porta of the Abbey should be called The Blackbirds (more correctly, the inn is The Three Blackbirds), and the nearby farm is Croes-y-mwyalch, the blackbirds' cross.

Around the Abbey itself are a number of stone statues, but these are on the boundary wall of a formal garden. Away in the wild part of the park, among the trees and bracken, is an old stone figure of a man, with a dog at his feet. I had always been told that this was Robin Hood, and he does have a horn, which might prove it, yet there is no obvious reason why Robin Hood should be calling his Merry Men from their rest in Llantarnam Park. Or did Friar Tuck live in the Monks' Cells? It was only recently that I saw, for the first time in print, that the statue is really supposed to be Robin Hood. I wonder. . . .*

Even the ghost of Llantarnam Park is a mystery. It is said to be a lady in white, and that is about all that is known—if that, in fact, is known. It is more likely that the supposed figure in white is a White Monk, for the Abbey was of the Cistercian Order, founded by Howel ap Iorwerth, Lord of Caerleon, in the reign of Henry II, in the twelfth century. One of the Priors, John ap Howell, was killed in 1405 at the Battle of Usk. After the dissolution, William Morgan, a grandson of Sir Thomas Morgan of Pencoed, and a son of John Morgan of Caerleon,

* I understand poor Robin Hood has fallen from his pedestal and is likely to be moved elsewhere. This has happened very recently.

purchased the Abbey lands in 1553, and also took into the estate the Abbey Grange, since known as Pentre Bach, which stands near the foot of Twyn Barllwm. Before the Morgans owned Pentre Bach the name mentioned in old documents was Cefn-vynach, or monks' ridge. William Morgan rebuilt the ruined Abbey, and while part of the present building incorporates the original, it is mainly Tudor, with later additions. Pentre Bach is predominantly Tudor and Jacobean, and is now a farm, and it is from the field path from Llantarnam that the age and some idea of its previous size can be gauged. Pentre Bach means "little village", so there must have been a splendour about the house in its early days.

There were Morgans at Llantarnam from the sixteenth century until the eighteenth, when the male line died out, leaving the inheritance to the female survivors. The same Morgan family owned Penrhos, near Caerleon, and Llansôr. The various residences all over the county were acquired for the numerous sons of each generation, often through the law of gavelkind, or equal inheritance.

From the top of the park, and looking towards Mynydd Maen, there is a sombre beauty of shadowed hills and a certain peace, and away towards Pontypool, in the valley, are the signs of tall chimneys, and they are too far away to detract from the scene. This is where the country gives way to industry. The Afon Llwyd flows turbulently through Llantarnam, down in the hollow, and before it reaches there it has come through tinplate towns, the brick works, and the land of iron, steel, and coal. (Llantarnam is thought to be derived from Llan Torfaen, Torfaen, or "breaker of stones", being the old name of the Afon Llwyd.) There is just a glimpse of industry from the park, while a slight turn brings the country into focus again. That is typical of Gwent, a county of infinite variety.

It is difficult to say what the immediate few miles around Cwmbran will look like in the future, for it is planned as a satellite town, spreading towards the mountain and towards Llantarnam, laid out by planners. There is a new plan for the centre of Newport, too, but no one can tell how long these schemes will take.

Although, perhaps, it is above Llantarnam that industry begins, at one time Ponthir, between Caerleon and Llantarnam, held a high place in the iron industry of this part of Gwent, and much of the power for the works was generated by the Afon Llwyd itself. Some of the famous names connected with iron were known as the proprietors of the works at Ponthir—Hamman Davis, the Hanburys, the Butlers (of Panteg), Richard Fothergill, in 1818, of the Sirhowy Works, his brother and his son, Thomas. Then the Moggridges of Blackwood, and David Grey from over the border at Maesteg. The works changed hands very frequently and closed altogether in the nineteenth century before being opened as tinplate works for Richards and Hopkins.

Tinplate and bricks are still manufactured in the comparatively rural area between Ponthir and Caerleon.

Beyond the gentle lanes of Henllys, and behind the spreading streets of Cwmbran, the country becomes a little harder, perhaps a transition between the rather more welcoming slopes of Twyn Barllwm and the industrialised hills farther up the valley. The lanes from Cwmbran are torn between the unyielding hills and the relentless push of industry, much of it old and deserted, and here and there along the lanes are terraces of anything from two to twenty small town houses in rural isolation.

Farther up the mountain are pretty woods, with beech and bluebells and numerous springs, and the Dowlais Brook which eventually runs into the Afon Llwyd between Llantarnam and Ponthir; and there are the cottages called Ty Pwca (pwca translating easily into "Puck", and meaning fairy, or "the little people"). Villages like Upper Cwmbran have more industrial dullness about them than country-cottage effect. Heavy industry leaves its mark in Cwm Afon.

About 1,000 feet up the mountainside is the old ruined church of Llanderfel, founded in the time of King Arthur by a great warrior, Derfel Gadarn, or Derfel the Strong, who towards the end of his life gave up his warlike ways and turned to religion. Somehow one expects this type of ancient story to be connected with the hillsides of Mynydd Maen, rather than the more factual historical incidents. Which reminds me of what David Williams wrote in the eighteenth century, about Twyn Barllwm, the tumulus on Mynydd Maen, though he was looking at it from Risca: "The artificial Hillock upon the high mountain near Risca, is commonly called, Tom Barlam; I conjecture this name to be a corruption of Tum-*ulus* Berthlan, some mighty Potentate in Wales, but know nothing about him." And neither do I.

Beneath the Mynydd Maen ridge, in the softer Henllys country, is Castell y Bwch. Bwch was a giant, and as his name is perpetuated, even though his castle has gone, there is no reason to disbelieve in his existence, especially as he had a number of sons who scattered themselves about the county and over the border into Glamorgan, and when we walk through the lovely Vale of Usk we will see where some of them settled. Bwch ended his days by having his head cut off, poor giant. There must have been a wife in the story somewhere, a veritable Amazon no doubt, and she must have been rather like the old woman who lived in a shoe with all those giant children about her.

But to come back to more mundane matters. In a diary kept in his younger days by an old resident of Maes-y-rhiw, near Cwmbran, are some of the details of life in a small industrial town in the eighteen-fifties. Henry Lawrence Morgan took up a position with the old Cwmbran Iron Works in 1852, and his diary is full of references to pig-iron and tinplate, but mostly of a purely contemporary nature and not of great interest to the present-day reader. In the middle of an entry relating to collecting cash at Abersychan, or rents at Caerleon, he tells of visiting his "mama", or staying with "Uncle John" in Newport, going to church, or conducting local choral societies; he then reverts to his daily work, which appears to have been taken with great earnestness. His diary begins in a deliberate fashion:

DIARY

1852, *November* 26th. I this day commenced keeping a Diary upon my appointment to the Cwmbrân Iron Works under Messrs Darby & Brown which I this day also entered upon. Messrs Darby & Brown were at Cwmbrân Colliery with Mr Lawrence when I arrived at the Works, did not see Messrs Darby & Brown. Made an arrangement with Elizabeth Morris to lodge & board with her for 12/- per week to have two rooms, Bed & sitting rooms, & to be absent on Sundays. 4£ per annum for Washing if taken.

Mr Lawrence is evidently John Lawrence of Llangibby Hunt fame, and who founded the ironworks at

Pontnewynydd in 1837. Several times the fact is mentioned in the diary that Mr Lawrence had gone hunting, and once Henry Morgan went with him to hunt with the Llangibby Pack, but the fox went away to Wentwood which was particularly unpleasant that day. (Before John Lawrence became Master of the Llangibby Hunt, he ran a pack of hounds, hunting hare as well as fox on Mynydd Maen and the Henllys Vale. This pack was known as the Cwmbran Harriers and originated with hounds from the old Risca pack, and which were, of course, accustomed to the Mynydd Maen country.)

Under the date of March 1st, 1854, a long entry in Mr Morgan's diary is recorded, being a mixture of personal and business items. Part of it read, "Newport, Abergavenny & Hereford Railway opened took 10 New Shares in Newport & Pontypool Railway. Chas. Morgan of Tredegar died aged 25 years same age as myself last birthday"; and in the same year the diarist tells of visiting a house where there were "Ladies making warm clothing for army in Crimea". He need not have worried unduly about the age of young Charles Morgan being the same as his own, as Henry Lawrence Morgan lived to be over eighty.

Perhaps the most interesting entries to read today are the wages of employees in the iron industry, and in one instance a list is given of wages paid to a new team of men taken on at the works:

1852, *December* 11*th*. Puddlers to have 2/- a day with Ballers and Ball Rollers, Carpenter 2/9, Underhands 1/6, Blacksmiths 2/6 & 1£ per Week, Strikers 1/8, Squeezers 2/-. Night Watchmen 2/-, Railmen 2/3, Engineers 3/-, Firemen 2/-, Siezer 1/-.

Among the blast furnaces of the Pontypool district it is a little disconcerting to find that the natives of Pontypool have been known as "butterflies". A certain process in the iron industry was found to give a similar appearance to Japanese lacquer work, and Pontypool Japanware became a most popular form of decoration to such articles as trays, screens, and vases, and it was in connection with this work that the Pontypool residents were known as "butterflies".

Thomas Allgood of Nottingham was employed by the Hanbury Ironworks at Pontypool in 1660, and it was he who instigated the making of Japanware, founding the firm of Allgoods of Pontypool, and later of Usk. Pieces of Japanware are now sought by collectors who like the Oriental-type designs on a black background. One branch of the firm eventually moved to Usk, when in 1761 two younger members of the Allgood family had a difference of opinion strong enough to split the partnership. By the nineteenth century the Midlands were competing in the market for ornamental work, and gradually business declined until it died, at Pontypool, in 1822, and went on until about 1860 at Usk, when it, too, expired.

I wonder if the name "butterflies" will be applicable again today? At Pontypool, or to be more exact, at Mamhilad (with its Roman road over the hills), against a wonderful background of hills and fields, is the factory of British Nylon Spinners, said to be the biggest factory under one roof in Europe. Strangely enough, this factory is not the sprawling mass one would imagine; it is really quite a dignified factory, and when one thinks of the delicate yarn that is made there, then indeed one can only liken it to butterflies. Though in actual fact nylon is very tough, and among its many uses, including the inevitable and excellent nylon stockings, are ropes, suiting, and

105

Christchurch and Church House
Kemeys Inferior

curtain material and about eighty different textile purposes in all.

Mamhilad is no distance from Pontymoile, where Hanbury's Ironworks were operating in the sixteenth century, so industry seems to have completed the circle here. In the sixteenth century the ironworks must have been a source of wonder and a new outlook for the future, while today the nylon yarn made at the fine factory spins endless possibilities of employment and textile progress for *our* future. Before the settling of the Hanburys in Pontypool, the ironworks were already in existence, and in 1425 the Grant family of Glamorgan were the owners. As early as 1588 there was a regular account kept of the sale of iron at Pontypool.

Although Pontypool did not develop to any great extent until the late eighteenth century, the ironworks were always prosperous, and in 1729 the Pen-y-garn Baptist Chapel was erected to meet the needs of a growing population. Nonconformism was strong in the Pontypool area, and a Baptist College at Trosnant, existing in 1736, strengthened the Baptist cause in the county.

Between Pontymoile and Mamhilad is Llanvihangel Pontymoile, which seems to have remained in the past in certain respects, with its old thatched inn, the Horse and Jockey, standing next to the church which gave up its Welsh services as late as 1870.

If one family alone made Pontypool prosperous—and other places joined in the prosperity too—then the family was that of Hanbury. Baldwins, and Partridge, Jones and John Paton, and Whiteheads are the big names of the district today, but the Hanburys and Pontypool will for ever be associated. The early Monmouthshire ironworks of the Hanburys included Monkswood and Abercarn as

well as Pontymoile. The Hanbury family originated in
Worcestershire, and later there was a Datchet line.
Richard Hanbury was from Datchet, and he was the first
of the Hanburys to be connected with South Wales. He
acquired the wire works at Tintern to begin with. His
connection with the county seems to have been through
some distant relatives, the Watkins family of Pontypool,
and gradually his possessions in Monmouthshire increased to include property at Abercarn and, in 1572, the
old ironworks of Estarvarney, near Monkswood, which
had belonged to the monks from Tintern and, at the
dissolution, the lands had been granted to Henry, second
Earl of Worcester. At that time property was the only
county connection with the Hanburys, as the family did
not reside in the area then.

Richard died in 1608, and amongst his bequests was
£30 to Bartholomew Pettingale (his clerk), and a mourn-
ing gown and ring of the same value. Hanbury had intro-
duced Bartholomew to South Wales, and he was the first
of the family to live in the district. At some time they lived
at Panteg, and both Pettingale Wood and Pettingale
Farm are named after the family.

Through lease and purchase the Hanbury iron connections grew, and in the seventeenth century Capel
Hanbury, a grandson of Richard, came to settle in Pontypool, and thus began the long association with Monmouthshire. Capel's eldest son was the famous Major
John Hanbury who improved many of the methods used
in the iron industry: he made great strides in tinning, and
also in the rolling of the material.

Major John began the building of Pontypool Park, and
it is mostly the eighteenth-century structure which stands
today, now a public building set in the open space and

playing-fields belonging to the town, with the old Grotto at the top of the hill. John Hanbury married twice, his first wife having no children and dying young. His second marriage brought him in contact with the influential world of the Marlboroughs. When the Park was being built, the famous Duchess of Marlborough, Sarah, presented Major Hanbury with the fine iron gates at the entrance. It was not until the beginning of the nineteenth century that the original stone gate posts were exchanged for ornamental iron pillars which were cast at Blaenavon.

In the Hanbury Chapel at Trevethin church is a long memorial telling, précis-fashion, the main story of Major Hanbury's life, Major John Hanbury, perhaps one of the most famous ironmasters of them all:

Here lies the body of *John Hanbury*, Esq.
of Pont-poole in the county of Monmouth,
Who by his great understanding and Humanity,
Made the People of this Place and Neighbourhood Rich
and Happy,
And they will tell their Children to lastest Posterity
That he was a Wise and Honest Man.
He was chosen in Eight Parliaments,
And was Knight of the Shire, for the County of
Monmouth at his Decease.
He was appointed by the Great Duke of Marlborough
One of the Executors of his last Will.
He married BRIDGET, Daughter of SR EDWARD AYSCOUGH
of Kelsey in the County of Lincoln,
By whom he left five sons, John, Capel, Charles, George
and Thomas.
He died on the 14th day of June 1734 in the 70th year of
his Age.

That third son, Charles, was the one whose fortune was inherited from Charles Williams of Caerleon, and became Charles Hanbury-Williams, and we shall meet him again at Coldbrook Park, near Abergavenny, because he left industrial Pontypool for Coldbrook, which was a condition of his inheritance. Again, in the later eighteenth century, another Hanbury was to take an additional name to his own for a similar reason, when Capel Hanbury Leigh began another phase of the family story.

A Victorian bard, William Williams, who, beside his prize poems, wrote for any occasion necessary, a kind of Poet Laureate of Gwent, in one of his poems "Jubilee Rejoicings in Pontypool Park", in honour of the Queen's Jubilee in 1887, finishes up with four lines which I quote without comment:

Three cheers for Gen'rous Hanbury, who the Park so
  freely lent,
And to our Gallant Fire Brigade, of which he's
  President:
Captain and Mrs Bevan joy, life cloudless and serene;
Peace and prosperity to all, good night, "God Save the
  Queen".

I am certain Mr Williams was genuinely moved to write those words, but I am not so sure he was not having a chuckle when he wrote of the competitive choirs at the same festivity:

They sing! Sopranos warble, shriek; altos and tenors
  blend;
Hark to the bassos lion-roar which seems the heavens to
  rend!

Trevethin church, the old parish church of Pontypool, where the name of Hanbury is prominent, is still in what might be termed a village, with its walk through the fields, its two inns, the Mason's Arms and the appropriately named Old Yew Tree, one each side of the churchyard. There is an enthusiastic team of bell-ringers, and there is an unusual solidity in this twelfth-century church, bearing much evidence of interior restoration. The brass-work on the heavy door shines with frequent cleaning, and the pews are dark and extremely solid with their large fleur-de-lis on each one. The benefactors of Trevethin have left their mark in a number of tangible ways, and it is only the exterior of the tower that bears any sign of age.

Because of its text, a memorial tablet in the nave has a quality of pathos, recording the deaths of two young men of the district, nephews of the incumbent of the parish, the Reverend Thomas Davies, in 1856. The two young men were the Reverend Thomas Davies, B.A., lecturer at Gelligaer School, who died on the 30th May, 1856, aged twenty-six years, and the Reverend W. R. Roberts, B.A., rector of a country parish, of the same age, who died a day after his cousin, on the 1st June, 1856. These events in themselves, surely caused by an epidemic, which would not be unusual in the eighteen-fifties, would be a little out of the ordinary, but the memorial tells of the young men, who were born within a few weeks of each other, that at the young men's deaths, their mothers, sisters, were widows, and that they were not only educated at the same school but went on to university together. They were ordained on one Sunday by the same bishop, "and in death they were not divided".

The steep road through Trevethin goes on to Little Mountain and the ridge of Garn-wen and the Holy Well, while on the other side of Cwm Afon, instead of climbing up to Trevethin, is Pontnewynydd across the black, thick

Afon Llwyd. The steelworks make their great, impersonal noise, and right in the valley is the pit which was the scene of a dreadful disaster some sixty years ago, and which is commemorated by a window in Trevethin church. This is the land of iron and coal, and the industries that depend on these raw materials. In 1792 the progress was sufficient to justify the passing of an Act for the building of a canal from Pontnewynydd to Newport, with an extending Act in 1797. Before the extending Act was passed, the Monmouthshire Canal Navigation Company constructed a railroad from Blaenavon to the canal at Pontnewynydd. Industrialisation had become permanent. Yet at Pentre-piod, only a short, steep climb from Pontnewynydd (Pentre-piod is the village of the magpies), foxes steal the poultry, and the air blows fresh. This is the curious mixture of isolation and industry to be found all the way through the valleys, the towns and villages crouched in the narrow valleys, with the mountain fastness of the farms and rural communities of the hills above them.

Old stories tell of fairies and ghosts along the road from Pontypool to Crumlin, and perhaps the best of them all is the story of Pwca 'r Trwyn. This Pwca was a particularly useful sprite, living at Pantygasseg, a farm not far along the mountain from Pontypool. He did all kinds of household tasks, until one day he became displeased and took an opportunity of moving to Trwyn, a farm on Mynyddislwyn. The way in which he moved his quarters is in doubt. One story says that a maidservant from the Trwyn went to Pantygasseg to collect a jug of barm, and his displeasure at some incident being so great, he jumped into the jug as well, and was carried back to the Trwyn. It seems a long way for a jug of barm to be fetched. The other story has a pleasant fantasy to it.

Pwca settled himself in the centre of a ball of wool and rolled from Pantygasseg to Trwyn, bowling along the valleys and up the slopes, being plainly visible to those watching his progress. The theory has been put forward that a certain chieftain of Pontypool was in hiding at Trwyn, away from his native hillside and his foes, and the fairy story was given out to keep the superstitious (and suspicious) neighbours from going too close to the farm and seeing or hearing more than was necessary. This chieftain's name was Howell, and as Pontypool is sometimes thought to be a corruption of Pont ap Howell, or Howell's Bridge, there is a foundation for the legend springing from truth. But that ball of wool story is a pleasant invention.

Trwyn means nose, and on Mynyddislwyn is Trwyn, a forward-jutting piece of mountain, and there must have been situated the Trwyn farm; I have also heard that Pwca 'r Trwyn was so known for his own long nose. But Pwca 'r Trwyn is a favourite story in Gwent, and seems to have his domicile in many old houses, and the versions of the story differ in detail.

Near Abersychan the woods are thick on the steep hillsides, good mixed woods, and there is some fertile-looking country along the lower slopes of Garn Clochdy. The village sports grounds, usually long and narrow, lie at the bottom of the mountains in whatever flat piece of field they can find, mostly parallel with the railway and the main road, for above the valley bottom the roads soon begin to climb. The whole of the valley from Abersychan on the one side, and Garndiffaith and Varteg on the other, seems to be remote from industry, then Blaenavon at the top of the valley dispels any idea that Cwm Afon is a valley of soft mountain scenery and fertile slopes.

You must get out of the town to see Blaenavon. Climb
through the streets, which seem to have recovered from
the pre-war depression, go on past the Workmen's Hall,
where films are shown, and plays, and recreation in many
forms is obtained. A full-length play festival held for a
week brings companies from many parts of the county,
from Glamorgan, and from Bristol to compete. Strind-
berg vies with Shaw at these festivals, and Coward is
probably thrown in for good measure and a little light
relief.

As you climb, for Blaenavon is built on the hills, you
will see the coal-tips in the valley, and pitheads, and great
slag-heaps. But go on, for as you climb you will see the
worst hovels you will ever see. The most deplorable
housing conditions I have seen are in Blaenavon by the old
derelict works. Three sides of a square are bordered by
dwellings which must surely be condemned: they are tiny
terraced cottages waiting for a storm to swamp them; they
lean together for support, and they look on to a bare yard.
Valley housing conditions are known to be bad in places,
but this is beyond comprehension, beyond decency. The
enlightened twentieth century, or the dark ages? It is
difficult to say. Farther up, and still climbing, you pass a
long, high building, derelict on the ground floor, and up
above, in the high first and second floors, behind tiny,
neatly curtained windows, people are living.

Go up again, beyond any houses, and then turn around
and look back over Blaenavon, and there it is, beginning to
suffer again, but trying to catch up with its new life.
There is a huge pyramid of slag, the Coity Mountains
opposite bristle with cranes, and down in the valley is the
town. In 1936 King Edward VIII made his famous tour
of the depressed areas, and Blaenavon was one of the

places he visited, and it must have looked dead enough then. Looking down from the heights, this valley is alive now, surrounded by the dark mountains which hold the wealth of a mining district. As long as these places are prosperous then there is a certain beauty in the austere surroundings, but once the prosperity goes, then the whole place is dead and dark. This view, to me, is magnificent. It is a large view: high mountains and deep valleys, wooded slopes in the distance and sullen industry below.

I have seen sheep cropping the grass in Blaenavon's churchyard, because the mountainsides feed the flocks, and the mountain roads lead into the towns and villages. This emphasises the proximity of industry and agriculture in the hills and valleys. I have looked down from Mynydd y Garn-gawr on to Blaenavon, and from close on hand have heard the bewildered bleatings of sheep and lambs being sheared and dipped at a little mountain farm. Still higher, where the bare wastes of open-cast mining make a stony desert of the mountain top, I have seen cattle sheltering from the heat of the June sun beneath a great piece of open-cast mechanism.

To see the complete deadness of the after-effects of open-cast mining on the bare mountain top is to feel the horror of what must be happening in the agricultural land of Worcestershire and farther north. The road from Blaenavon to Brynmawr (this hilltop town with its wide square is just over the Border into Brecknock) passes the open-cast sites, and then suddenly the Sugar Loaf and the ranges of the Black Mountains can be seen from the bare heights of the Blorenge range. The range of mountains where the 1,834-foot Blorenge is the highest point is partly ravaged by desolate open-cast sites, and partly

heather-covered moorland. Looking across the moorland
is like looking across a windswept seacoast: there is such
distance, and somewhere there should be the sound of the
sea. Instead, in summer, there is the endless song of
larks.

In the first years of the nineteenth century three
hundred and fifty men were employed at Blaenavon
Works, and as some sort of railways were then beginning
to take the place of pack-mules it is worth quoting William
Coxe's contemporary witnessing of the making of one of
these tramways, or railroads. After all, the Coronation
Scot is descended in a direct line from such local en-
deavours.

"In the vicinity of Blaenavon we observed the process
of making a rail road, so called because it is formed by a
kind of frame with iron rails, or bars, laid lengthways,
and fastened or cramped by means of cross bars. The
ground being excavated, about six feet in breadth, and
two in depth, is strewed over with broken pieces of
stone, and the frame laid down; it is composed of rails,
sleepers, or cross bars, and under sleepers. The rail is a
bar of cast iron, four feet in length, three inches thick,
and one and a half broad; its extremities are respectively
concave and convex, or in other words are morticed
and tenanted into each other, and fastened at the ends
by two wooden pegs to a cross bar called the sleeper.
This sleeper was originally of iron, but experience
having shown that iron was liable to snap or bend, it is
now made of wood, which is considerably cheaper, and
requires less repair. Under each extremity of the
sleeper is a small piece of wood, called the under sleeper,
to which it is attached by a peg. The frame being thus

laid down and filled with stones, gravel, and earth, the iron rails form a ridge above the surface, over which the wheels of the cars glide by means of iron grooved rims three inches and a half broad.

"This is the general structure of the road when carried in a strait line; at the junction of two roads, and to facilitate the passage of two cars in opposite directions, moveable rails, called turn rails, are occasionally used, which are fastened with screws instead of pegs, and may be pushed sideways. The level of the ground is taken with great exactness, and the declivity is in general so gentle as to be almost imperceptible: the road, sometimes conveyed in a strait line, sometimes winding round the sides of precipices, is a picturesque object, and the cars filled with coals or iron, and gliding along occasionally without horses, impress the traveller, who is unaccustomed to such spectacles, with pleasing astonishment. The expense of forming· these roads is very considerable, varying according to the nature of the ground, and the difficulty or facility of procuring proper materials; it is seldom less than a thousand pounds per mile, and sometimes exceeds that sum.

"The cars, from the solidity of their structure, and the quantity of iron used in the axle tree and wheels, when loaded weigh not less than three tons and a half; they are drawn by a single horse, and the driver stands on a kind of footboard behind, and can instantaneously stop the car by means of a lever and a drop, which falls between the wheels, and suspends their motion. In places where the declivity is more rapid than usual, the horse is taken out, and the car impelled forward by its own weight."

About this time Thomas Hill and Samuel Hopkins were developing Blaenavon, whereas before, the Hanburys were taking the iron ore for manufacturing at Pontypool, and leaving the coal resources at Blaenavon untouched. In 1836 the Kennard family took over the ironworks, and still later a Quaker family from Birmingham, the Harfords, became the proprietors. It is the old Blaenavon Works which are still in existence and giving a certain amount of anxiety as to their future.

Percy Gilchrist, a chemist at Cwm Afon Works, moved in the early eighteen-seventies to the Blaenavon Works, and carried out experiments in his leisure hours on the making of steel. His cousin, Sidney Gilchrist Thomas, a London police clerk, was responsible for the idea, and Gilchrist worked on the experimental side of the job.

This type of experiment had successfully begun in 1856, when Henry Bessemer originated his process of converting molten pig-iron into steel, with the impurities removed. Eleven years later William Siemens discovered a method of steel production of an even finer quality, but this proved expensive. The Thomas-Gilchrist method, perfected in 1878 at Blaenavon, produced steel cheaply and on a large scale. Even iron with a high phosphorus content could be used with their method, and using either the Bessemer converters or the Siemens-Martin plant. The young cousins revolutionised the steel industry.

Over the mountain road to Llanfoist is Garn-ddyrys, where, in the eighteen-fifties, the material for the Crumlin Viaduct was produced. At the junction of this road and the one going to Pwll-du is Pen-fford-gôch Pond, one of the larger ponds found among the bog and heather of the mountain tops. There always seems to me to be something bottomless and uncanny about these ponds.

There are tracks across the mountains—if you know them—but the rough road a couple of hundred feet below the rocky summit of the Blorenge is a good one to use on the way to Llanelen, and then on to Abergavenny. The dark mass of the Blorenge from the Usk Valley does not look particularly inviting, but to go to Blaenavon and to walk down into the Usk Valley is a pleasant experience. The heather grows high each side. In early summer patches of palest green fern light up the dark of the heather, and tiny butterflies fly about, which I imagine to be some species of fritillary. The silence, save for the larks' song, is a tremendous thing on the flat of this high mountain. When the road begins to drop it is still a long way to the Vale of Usk, but it is very beautiful all around.

There is a great change in the country from Blaenavon, over the moors where the sheep and horses roam and the views are breathtaking, then down into the fertile Vale of Usk and the distant sight of the Black Mountains. But where am I? Certainly not in Cwm Afon. Back to Blaenavon we must go—Blaenavon, literally the end of the Afon—the dark torrent of the Afon Llwyd.

Chapter IV

THE USK VALLEY

Far in the valley where the heat haze lies,
And roads are whiter than a wood dove's wings,
Usk swirls 'neath Kemeys bridge and gently sings
    Of cool wet blueness caught from summer skies.
Softly the river's lullaby
Lilts through the shallows, and where pools are deep
It croons to old Llancayo, drowsed with sleep
    Of all the golden magic of July.

Myfanwy Haycock, from "July".

THE very name of Usk is derived from the old word for water, "Wysg", and as well as the history, natural and social, that lives within the Usk Valley, it is the water itself, the river, which has brought the district much of its renown. The tidal Usk, with one of the highest spring tides in the world, is a river famous for its trout and salmon. (The tidal river brings with it a tendency to floods, and around Usk there are "flood routes" going over high ground, and marked by signposts accordingly.) There are, too, the far-reaching tributaries of the Usk; there are castles, fields, and woods; there is history and there are horse-shows; there are market towns and villages, and wonderfully quiet lanes. It has everything one can wish for.

Newport has a chapter to itself, so I will start the journey of the Usk at ancient Caerleon.

I suppose Caerleon-on-Usk is known more for its history than anything else, and Caerleon was a centre for foreign trade before the Romans came, and must have been, for that alone, an attraction to the Romans.

Shipping made its way there until Newport took over its importance. There are Iron Age forts near Caerleon, and stories of King Arthur and his Knights of the Round Table. In the twelfth century Howel ap Iorwerth was Lord of Caerleon, and later there were the Tudors who built there; during Elizabeth's reign the shipping declined. History and legend are mixed up: it is difficult to know what is truth, half-truth, or mythical tale.

From A.D. 75 to 412 the Romans were at Caerleon (Isca Silurum), and the Roman remains are extensive, and as for pieces of pottery, coins, and relics of a past civilisation, they are numberless. The red Samian ware, imported from Gaul, is well in evidence. The Second Augusta Legion was stationed at Isca, Julius Frontinus commanding the garrison: he was also the ruler of Roman Britain from A.D. 73 until about A.D. 78, when he was succeeded by Creous Julius Agricola. The amphitheatre is outside the city to the south-west. The excavations have found a huge arena, the exits and seating accommodation clearly shown, and everything much as it was during the occupation. There is a little museum at Caerleon containing Samian ware, inscribed stones, domestic impedimenta, burial urns, and many other treasures of Roman life. Incidentally, this year marks the one hundredth anniversary of the opening of this museum, an historical record in itself. In the basement of the pilastered building are stone coffins and mosaic floor-work.

It seems that almost every time the ground is turned at Caerleon a fresh coin is unearthed or a piece of pottery found; this might be on the Bulmoor road, or as far afield as Tredunnock, which was an outpost of the garrison. The Roman garrison was well-established, and the population must have been large to provide such

Newbridge-on-Usk
Pencoed Castle

evidence of its being. It is more than likely that the old forts such as Lodge Hill, once cleared of the Silures, were used by the Romans as additional defence and as outposts between the towns of Burrium (Usk) and Gobannium (Abergavenny). Not only was Isca strategically well placed, but it had access to the iron and coal resources of South Wales.

The fame of the facts known of the Roman occupation is closely contested by the Arthurian legend. King Arthur and his Knights, and the Seer, Merlin, are as much part of Caerleon as the more tangible evidence of Roman life. One old history book says, "Arthur, after his Coronation at Caerleon, which he had retaken from the Saxons", and goes on to say, "Arthur was undoubtedly a great General. It is a pity his Actions have serv'd for Foundation to number-less Fables, that have been publish'd concerning him: whereas his life was worthy of being recorded by the gravest and most able Pen." But romance has always surrounded Arthur's life, and his death too, since Geoffrey of Monmouth wrote *The Histories of the Kings of Britain* in the early part of the twelfth century. It was Geoffrey who really aroused interest in Arthur, but some centuries before that Nennius had written of him. Since that time various writers have written in prose and verse of the Court of King Arthur.

By 1470 Sir Thomas Malory had written his *Morte d'Arthur*, a prose work divided into numerous short sections. The Court of the King moves between Cornwall and Wales, but Caerleon was the scene of Arthur's coronation: "Then the king moved into Wales, and let cry a great feast that it should be holden at Pentecost after the incoronation of him at the city of Carlion."

Thomas Churchyard, the sixteenth-century poet, wrote

121

Llanmartin Church
Old Chepstow

at some length, and less crudely, on the Arthurian legend, and, like Malory, he described the coronation at Caerleon:

> King Arthur sure was crowned there,
>   It was his royall seate:
> And in this towne did sceptre beare,
>   With pompe and honour greate.

He goes on:

> The citie reacht to Greetchurch then,
> And to Saint Gillyans both:

Greetchurch is Christchurch, on the hill above Caerleon, and there is a marginal note about St Julian's, in which Churchyard says, "A faire house where Sir William Herbert dwelles".

In the fourth song of Michael Drayton's *Polyolbion*, published in 1622, he tells of Arthur defeating his enemies in all countries.

Tennyson's *Idylls of the King* is full of "Old Caerleon". The Forest of Dean must, in Tennyson's opinion, have included Wentwood, for surely it is Wentwood that he means in "The Marriage of Geraint":

> For Arthur on the Whitsuntide before
> Held court at old Caerleon upon Usk.
> There on a day, he sitting high in hall,
> Before him came a forester of Dean,
> Wet from the woods, with notice of a hart
> Taller than all his fellows, milky-white,
> First seen that day: these things he told the King.
> Then the good King gave order to let blow
> His horns for hunting on the morrow morn.

That this is Wentwood is borne out later in the narrative,

122

when Guinevere, lost in sweet dreams of Lancelot, forgot the hunt,

> But rose at last, a single maid with her,
> Took horse, and forded Usk, and gain'd the wood.

The slopes of Wentwood come down to the banks of the Usk on the opposite side from Caerleon village.

For part of his stay in Caerleon, Tennyson stayed at the Hanbury Arms, which has been modernised inside, but from the bridge, the inn, with its long wall down to the river, retains its style, which is somewhere in the region of four or five hundred years old. Until very recently an old dog spit was still in place over the fireplace, but the interior character, to a certain extent, has gone.

The Bull is another inn which from the outside gives promise of a Tudor interior, but this fancy is soon removed. The Bull Inn stands in the Square, one of the windows positively squinting with age, but most of the interior has been "renovated" or removed. The name is taken from the arms of the Morgans who lived at the house in the sixteenth century. John Morgan, who was a younger son of the Morgans of Langstone and Pencoed, owned the house and the old Priory opposite until he died in 1525. The bulls' heads were the arms of Bledri, an ancestor of Llewelyn ap Ivor, the father of the first of the Morgan line. Quite inexplicably there is a Medusa's head in an upstairs wall. There is also a room which is known to exist but cannot be found. In an upstairs room, too (the same room where there should be an old fireplace, but which is now boarded up), is the loft where the "secret passage" begins. It runs right down through the house, underneath the road to the Priory cellars.

The Priory, presumably founded in the twelfth century

by the Lord of Caerleon, Howel ap Iorwerth, he who founded the Cistercian Abbey at Llantarnam, has been a private house since 1450, when John Morgan was the owner. Morgans remained at the Priory until 1835, when the line died out. It is the Tudor influence which remains at the Priory, but the cellars are believed to be part of the original twelfth-century building. The passage to The Bull is blocked in these cellars, but the archway over the bricks marks the opening. The rooms of the Priory are very spacious, and not too large for modern life, a well-planned residence indeed. The long windows look over the garden and a field towards the amphitheatre. The house is built squarely around a courtyard known as the Nuns' Court, and a passage surrounds the square inside. The fifteenth-century windows overlooking the Nuns' Court from this passage are delightful, with small paintings of Roman leaders and finely written verses about each one. I imagine these windows to be unique.

The Charity School near the church was founded by Charles Williams, who died in 1720. When he was a young man he killed his cousin, Edmund Morgan, of Penllwyn, in a duel at Caerleon, and to escape the consequences he fled to Smyrna, where he made a fortune before returning to this country. He was helped in his escape by a friend, John Hanbury, the ironmaster of Pontypool, and became godfather to Hanbury's son. This godchild inherited the Williams' fortune, and also the name, which was the origin of the family of Hanbury-Williams, who we will know more intimately when we reach Coldbrook Park, near Abergavenny.

Another member of the Hanbury family, one of the several Capel Hanburys, had ironworks at Abercarn, and after some difference of opinion his Abercarn manager,

John Griffiths, left Capel Hanbury to set up an iron-works at Caerleon, on the Ponthir road. This was in 1749.

Shipping has left Caerleon, and one can hardly call it industrial. The brickworks and tinplate works between Caerleon and Ponthir remain, but have been there so long that they become part of the scenery. Caerleon is busy with its various occupations, rural and industrial, and does not live in the past consciously, although there is enough history bounded by its Roman walls if it never makes history again.

The Afon Llwyd knows the ways of industry, as we have already seen, before it joins the Usk at Caerleon, but it becomes part of the rural scene between Llantarnam and Llanfrechfa. One of its streams is the Candwr, and another smaller tributary of the Usk is the Soar, and where they and numerous springs and streams add their music the troubles of industry and history seem to have passed by. This is the kind of country to be in when there is no object in view save to be in the country—which is by far the nicest way of doing things. Roughly, the area is that bounded by the main road from Caerleon to Usk, right around to Pontypool, and back down to Caerleon, through Llanfrechfa. The Berthin Brook, nearer Usk, completes the fertility of this land. I know there are times in summer when the Llandegfedd people and those living throughout the area are unable to find water coming from the pumps and roadside taps, but in the winter and early spring the whole place seems to me to be running with water. The ditches are full, the springs drip into them from the hedges, and the stones in the tracks sink into the mud as you walk. The lanes stop in mid-air around here, or, at least, they lead to farms and no farther;

they go uphill and downhill and turn about, and as you walk there is a stream burbling along with you.

Michael Drayton, in his *Polyolbion,* was impressed by the Usk's tributaries:

With all her wat'ry train, when now at last she came
Unto that happy Town which bears her only name,
Bright Birthin, with her friend Olwy, kindly meet her:
Which for her present haste, have scarcely time to
    greet her:
But earnest on her way, she needsly will be gone;
So much she longs to see the ancient Carleon.

There are woods, too, and around the Sluvad and all the other coverts there are foxes. This is part of the Llangibby Hunt country. The foxes are such a menace here that there are fox shoots organised by farmers, particularly around Glascoed, and they go, with a collection of terriers, and sometimes a couple of foxhounds, to thick woods where the Hunt is unable to reach. The Llangibby hounds originated probably several hundred years ago, being reinforced by John Lawrence's own pack when he became Master in the middle of the nineteenth century.

At Caerleon, in 1862, Arthur Machen was born, son of the Reverend Jones, and before he went to London and became a journalist, taking a name of Gwent to find his fame, he lived most of his youth at Llandewi Rectory, and he always loved that quiet corner of Gwent. In his book *Far Off Things* he wrote:

"I shall always esteem it as the greatest piece of fortune that has fallen to me, that I was born in that noble, fallen Caerleon-on-Usk, in the heart of Gwent.

My greatest fortune, I mean, from that point of view which I now more especially have in mind, the career of letters. For the older I grow the more firmly am I convinced that anything which I may have accomplished in literature is due to the fact that when my eyes were first opened in earliest childhood they had before them the vision of an enchanted land. As soon as I saw anything I saw Twyn Barlwm, that mystic tumulus, the memorial of peoples that dwelt in that region before the Celts left the Land of Summer. This guarded the southern limit of the great mountain wall in the west; a little northward was Mynydd Maen— the Mountain of Stone—a giant, rounded billow; and still to the north mountains, and on fair, clear days, one could see the pointed summit of the Holy Mountain by Abergavenny. It would shine, I remember, a pure blue in the far sunshine; it was a mountain peak in a fairy tale. And then to eastward the bedroom window of Llandewi Rectory looked over hill and valley, over high woods, quivering with leafage like the beloved Zacynthus of Ulysses, away to the forest of Wentwood, to the church tower on the hill above Caerleon. Through a cleft one might see now and again a bright yellow glint of the Severn Sea, and the cliffs of Somerset beyond. And hardly a house in sight in all the landscape, look where you would. Here the gable of a barn, here a glint of a whitewashed farm-house, here blue wood smoke rising from an orchard grove, where an old cottage was snugly hidden; but only so much if you knew where to look. And of nights, when the dusk fell and the farmer went his rounds, you might chance to see his lantern glimmering a very spark on the hillside. This was all that showed in a vague, dark world; and the only sounds were the faint distant barking of the sheepdog and the melancholy cry of the owls from the border of the brake."

Llandewi Fach and Llandegfedd, with their little churches, one on the hill and one in the hollow, without spire or steeple, but each with a bell turret to call the people across the fields and down the lanes. Both churches were rebuilt in the late nineteenth century, in a similar style to the original twelfth-century buildings, although certain portions of the older buildings remain. Llandegfedd takes its name from St Tegfydd, who was the mother of Teilo, Bishop of Llandaff. She was murdered by the pagan Saxons in the fifth century, and martyred as an upholder of the Christian religion. Llandewi is dedicated to the national saint, Dewi, or David.

The lane narrows near Llandegfedd church, and it is either a case of fording the Soar or crossing it by the little wooden bridge.

This is country where the beauty lies in the nearness of the birds, the hedgerows, and the streams. The architecture here is not of castles and churches, but the domestic architecture of small farms, and the beautiful Llansôr house, quite unlike any other house of its kind I know. It has such mellowness and dignity of design. The Meyricks, descended from Rhys Goch, a Welsh prince, and father of Gwladys, who married Ynyr, King of Gwent in the sixth century, lived at Llansôr until the seventeenth century, when Mary Meyrick, the heiress, married a William James, and the family continued in possession until 1885.

Another old building with long-standing connections is the other Llansôr—Llansôr Fawr—in one of the

128

Chepstow Castle

Morgan strongholds around Llanhennock. In the six-teenth century Thomas Prosser lived there, and his grand-daughter, Catherine, married one of Edward Morgan's sons from Llantarnam, George. The old house eventually descended to Florence, daughter of Edmund Morgan of Penllwyn. Florence was the wife of John Jones, of Llanarth, and that family held Llansôr Fawr until 1843.

So both Llansôr and Llansôr Fawr had a long record of family life, and they retain a comfortable, mellow beauty today.

Between Llanfrechfa and Llandegfedd there is a steep path, and before it climbs again there is a pretty bridge over the Candwr, then the hedges are close each side and the tree-tops meet overhead, and it is like walking through a tunnel, while underfoot there are stones, and the width is only for one to walk.

One Christmas morning I went to early morning Communion at Llanfrechfa church. There was little light as we crossed by the field path from Llantarnam, and it was cold, but when we came from the church among the trees, with the sound of laughter and greetings, the red sun was rising, and the frost was showing white—and it really was Christmas.

Llangibby is part of the country between Caerleon and Usk, but it lies on the main road, not tucked away like Llandegfedd and Llandewi. A sixth-century saint, Cybi (of North Wales), gives it its name, which correctly is Llangybi. The ancient name of the village was Tregrug, or "place on the mount". The old castle ruin is on high ground, while the present house, also known as Llangibby Castle, is built just below this mound. From the road to Common Coed-y-Paen the house, and the

9*   129

Inner Court, Chepstow Castle

woodland behind it, is seen in great beauty, while down below is the village itself, with the wide sweep of Wentwood on the other side of the river.

The manor of Llangibby descended with the lordship of Usk, Caerleon, and Trellech. In 1545 Roger Williams purchased the Priory lands of Usk, which included the Llangibby estates, and it was Roger who first built a house below the earlier castle, though the present house was probably built after the Civil War. Among the estates purchased by Roger Williams was Cefn-Ila, which at the end of the sixteenth century was used by his second son, William. (Cefn-Ila was later to be the home of Edward John Trelawney, friend of Byron and Shelley, and at one time a privateer as well as an author.) In 1707 the castle was enhanced by the addition of an avenue of trees planted to the river, and there are trees now from the main road to the river still in orderly procession.

A famous turncoat during the Civil War was Sir Trevor Williams, who began as a loyal subject of the King, but later threw in his lot with Parliament, and was arrested by order of King Charles. He was released, presumably owing to his previous allegiance to the Crown, in return for which leniency he again joined the Roundheads, with some success, as he took Monmouth, then Usk, and helped in the siege of Raglan. Some time later he is noted taking Chepstow with Nicholas Kemeys, his uncle, for the King. As the fortunes of war changed, so did the loyalties of Sir Trevor. At the Restoration he took out a pardon, regained his estates, and in peaceful times was a Member of Parliament for the county.

In 1749 the Williams line might have ended, as the male line died, leaving a daughter, Ellen. However, when Ellen married William Addams, his name was added to her own, and thus began the family of Addams-Williams.*

The church contains memorials to many of the family, including the gentleman of divided loyalties, Sir Trevor Williams. This is a typical cartouche of its age, with a small skull and crossbones at the base, while the inscription is black and neat and closely written.

Beneath the whitewashing of the interior of the well-proportioned church, the Commandments have been found, painted upon the stones in the nave, while in the chancel is a design or writing just discernible. It is thought that the chancel murals are of much greater age than the supposed Puritan work in the nave. Adam of Usk, fourteenth-century cleric and historian, held the living of Llangibby at one time.

Although several houses between Llanhennock and Tredunnock, overlooking the river, were Morgan residences, it is Garn Fawr, owned by a Pencoed Morgan in 1581, which retains its Elizabethan dignity and beauty. The house takes its name from garn (or carn), a cromlech, and was built in the twelfth century originally, on the site of a house belonging to Thomas, son of Iddon, King of Gwent in the sixth century, from whence he took his name, Thomas o'r Garn.

I heard a nice story about the Garn at that most friendly of inns, the White Hart, Llangibby (this old house belonged to the Commandery of the Knights of Jerusalem). Ellis, the postman, who likes modern houses —old ones, he says, give him the creeps—told me that there is a passage from Garn Fawr running beneath the river to Kemeys House on the opposite bank, from there

* The house is now to be demolished. This year has seen the end of too many old landmarks in the county (October 1950).

to Chapel Farm, Llandevaud, and from the farm on to Pencoed Castle. That story I imagine to be about as tall as the passage is long: about as accurate as a country mile. Then I begin to wonder—have I not heard of a passage at the Garn? Pencoed Castle? Is there not a secret passage there? These old stories run away with the imagination, yet . . .

From Usk to Caerleon the river twists its way between the flat fields near Llangibby, then through the softly rising country from Newbridge to Llanhennock on the one bank, while on the other side are the slopes of Wentwood and that lovely country around Llantrissent and Llan-llowell (there is a cottage here with a riotous display of lupins), where a steep lane goes through Llewellyn's Dingle, climbing and twisting, and eventually dropping down into Llangwm. In the autumn the trees from the woods shower the valley below with their leaves, and somehow, in the lane between, it is sheltered from the leaf-storm. This is beautiful country, with its mountain views and its solitude.

William Gilpin, on his 1770 tour, liked the winding ways of the Usk:

"Through this kind of road we passed many miles. The Usk continued, everywhere, our amusing companion: and if, at any time, it made a more devious curve, than usual, we were sure to meet it again, at the next turn."

It is difficult to classify Llangwm and the villages near, because while it is surrounded by tributaries of the Pill and Olway Brooks, and the Pill and Olway themselves (which are the Usk's flourishing children), its character is perhaps mingled with the sweeping country between Usk and Chepstow, where Wentwood's spurs and woods crouch on the one side, and the Chepstow Park Wood (once part of Wentwood's Royal Chase) flourishes on the other. The great fort of Gaer-Llwyd and other tumuli are near, and the country is like the Wye Valley without the river, with wooded slopes and a certain grandeur.

Llangwm's eleventh-century church is at the end of a lane, tucked out of sight in a hollow (as its name suggests), and there its treasure is hidden. There is another little church next to the Pentre farm, but to find the rood screen of Llangwm, which is one of the few left in the county, it is necessary to go on to the hollow where the stream runs and the trees make a cool gloom. There is a real age about the exterior of this church, while in the chancel restorers have made away with any sign of an early existence. The screen and loft of Llangwm are about five hundred years old, and have not only escaped the destruction of the restorers but the earlier ravages of Cromwell's men. The work is executed in a light-coloured wood in a series of designs, culminating in the intricacies of the loft, or balustrade, with the background of the open-work coloured in blue, green, and red, the latter colours being pale and not strident primary colours. If this is local work, then there were certainly fine craftsmen in the district.

An unusual feature is the link with pre-Christian human sacrifice, or fertility rites. On the corbels of the chancel arch, behind the screen, weird heads are carved, with oak-leaves sprouting from their mouths. Each corbel bears a different design, the one with a face on the two rounded corners, the other showing a larger face the width of the corbel. The oak leaves were a Druidical symbol, and there must be some connection between the corbels and the ancient rites which were, in part, often incorporated into the Christian belief.

The Cradocks and the Gwyns were the two main families of the Llangwm area from the early seventeenth century to the eighteenth century, and among the Cradocks, who lived at Trevela, the house built around a great tree, and still in existence, was Walter Cradock, a staunch upholder of the early nonconformist religion, and who succeeded William Wroth as minister at Llanvaches. Ty-Fry, quite close to Trevela, was the Gwyns' home, and also the Pwll, purchased by John Gwyn in 1652. The two families were united in marriage, when Joan, daughter of William Cradock of Trevela, married John Gwyn, and the name Cradock Gwyn is found among later members of the family. In fact, Cradock was used by many of the collateral branches for their sons' names.

Trevela means town of the wolves, or wolf-town, and not far away, on the other side of the prehistoric camp, Gaer-fawr, is Wolvesnewton, with its church dedicated to St Thomas à Becket, but founded as early as 1188 by the lord of the manor, sir Fwniel. The connection with wolves is a strange one in this district, for while the animals were found in the Forest of Wentwood and in the wooded and hilly country around Wolvesnewton, the chief family of this village, from the first to the sixteenth centuries, was that of Wolf, who came originally with the Romans, settled, and became part of the Gwent countryside's pattern. The old Welsh name for the village of Wolvesnewton has no connection with the Wolfs or the wolves, being Tre-newydd-dan-y-gaer, the new town under the fort.

From all the outlying farms and villages the 'buses take the people into Usk, that busy, cheerful town, with its Twyn Square, full of 'buses, coming and going to and from rural areas, and, via Pontypool, to the industrial valleys. Usk (Roman Burrium), with its Three Salmons Hotel, its two Glamorgan county cricketers, its Agricultural College, its castle, and, of course, its fishing.

An early visitor to Usk, Thomas Churchyard, in the sixteenth century, wrote of Usk's salmon, and of the town, in complimentary manner:

A Pretie towne, calde Oske neere Raggland stands,
A river there, doth beare the self same name:
His christall streams, that runnes along the sands,
Shewes that it is, a river of great fame.
Fresh water sweete, this goodly river yeelds,
And when it swels, it spreads ore all the feelds:
Great store of fish, is caught within this flood,
That doth indeed, both towne and countrey good.

A thing to note, when sammon sailes in Wye,
(And season there: goes out as order is)
That still of course, in Oske doth sammons lye,
And of good fish, in Oske you shall not mis.
And this seemes straunge, as doth through Wales appere,
In some one place, are sammons all the yeere:
So fresh, so sweete, so red, so crimp withall,
That man might say, loe, sammon here at call.

The pollution of the Usk by the Afon Llwyd (reckoned to be one of the dirtiest rivers in Wales) is a danger, but above this confluence the Usk is a clean river, a trout and salmon river, while dace and roach are taken in the winter months. The river is free from the trout-devouring pike, which makes it superior to the Wye for the trout-fisherman. Probably the record for size was the salmon caught in a net in 1782, which weighed 68½ lb. A 43 lb.

salmon has been caught recently by rod (in 1949, not a very good year), though the largest rod-and-line salmon to be caught was a 48-pounder in 1913. In 1880 Alfred Crawshay of Llanfair caught twenty-eight spring-run salmon in a day.

The trout caught in the Usk are anything from $\frac{1}{2}$ to 6 lb., though 3 lb. is a fairly common weight. In 1935 one was caught at $9\frac{1}{4}$ lb.

Much of the Usk fishing is available for visitors near Usk itself and at Abergavenny and at various places along the banks, sometimes the rights being held by the innkeepers and sometimes by farmers. Especially are the rights held by farmers in the trout streams of the Pill and Olway.

The name Harry Powell is synonymous with fishing in Usk, and probably wherever fishing is the talk. Now it is the late Harry Powell, but his shop trades under the old name and is run by a lady who was taught fly-tying by Mr Powell himself. This lady is the wife of Lionel Sweet, of Usk, Captain of the Welsh Trout Fishing Team, and European and British champion of so many events. Mr Sweet is perhaps better known as a tournament fly-caster, and there are not many records that he has not held and, in fact, holds now: he once made a cast of 69 yards at an exhibition. I have never seen a casting tournament, but Mr Sweet once became engrossed showing me the wrist movements used in casting—with a poker for want of a rod. I expected a trout to be swimming in the fireplace at any moment.

Coxe dismisses Usk Castle ruins as "neither magnificent, nor highly interesting in their appearance", but they have certainly been ruined at moments of great importance in Border history. The de Clares were the first known owners of Usk Castle, and it seems likely that they built the fortress, as there was no mention of it in Domesday, but soon afterwards the de Clares, Lords of Pembroke, were recorded as its owners.

Bwch, the giant, comes in here again, as he had a son called Buga, and the old name for Usk was Castell Bryn Buga, so perhaps Buga lived here before the Clares. Several other brothers were settled in the Vale of Usk, so why not Buga?

Gilbert de Clare, known as Strongbow for his great strength and prowess as an archer, was likely to have been the founder of the Priory at Usk. When he died in 1148 he was buried at Tintern Abbey, which was also of his founding. His third son, Walter, was Lord of Caerwent.

Among the various occupiers of Usk were the Mortimers, and also Simon de Montfort held it for a very short time during the comings and goings of battle. Usk, with Caerleon and Newport, was burnt by Glyndwr's forces, but in 1403, when the battle went ill for him, his son was taken prisoner and his army routed. It was during this battle of Usk that the Abbot of Llantarnam, John ap Howell, was killed, a believer in Glyndwr's cause. The castle eventually passed from the Crown into the ownership of the Herbert family by way of William ap Thomas, first Earl of Pembroke, and finally to the Beauforts.

In 1899 *The Times* became disturbed by the prospective fate of Usk Castle. Under the heading of "The Monmouthshire Ruins of the Beauforts", and after an historical description of the castle, the extract went on:

"At a recent sale some singular suggestions were made as to the future of the venerable pile which can boast such a history. The auctioneer seemed in doubt whether it might be more fittingly used as a water tower for the supply of the town or as a kind of *café chantant* for the entertainment of excursionists."

The nearest I have been to seeing the castle used as a *café chantant* was at a performance of *Hamlet* set on the green within the walls, with the king's ghost appearing greyly over the battlements—a most fitting setting.

The first Charter was granted to Usk in 1398 by Roger Mortimer, Earl of March, but the document was destroyed during one of Glyndwr's routs. The ratification of the original Charter was made by Edmund de Mortimer in 1416. The township of Usk was governed by a Portreeve, who was elected by the burgesses. The Portreeve, who acted as president of the Corporation, also presided at the Courts Leet, where criminals were tried, usually for minor offences, but occasionally for crimes of some social magnitude; their powers declined somewhat in later years. The ancient office of Portreeve, and its attendant council of burgesses, continued until 1885, when some standardisation of local government was forming. With such a long record of township, no wonder Usk retains an air of independence and prosperous solidity.

The de Clares founded the Priory of Usk, and also the Priory Church, but the building of the priory existed after the Dissolution until about 1869, when it was pulled down, leaving only the old gateway, and very little more. In September 1950 the building was burnt down. One part of the old Priory now in existence, but at Cefn Tilla Court, is a frieze bearing thirty heraldic designs, probably of various owners of the manor of Usk. In the church itself is a brass, some four to five hundred

years old, commemorating Adam of Usk, historian and
cleric. But the stone which gives a human side to the
historical picture, and life to the idea of the adventurous
Elizabethans, is the one with a sword cut down the side,
and the figure four inscribed backwards each time it is
used:

> Watter Iones I doe him
> Prayse A valiant souldiour
> in his days unto the Wars
> would he goe to fight aga
> inst his forraine foe to
> advaunce a pike before his Queene
> the which Elisabeth have
> seen his sword and speare
> he did advaunce and then he
> took his way to Fraunce and
> landed in the ile of ree;
> where his desire was to bee
> and to the lord he gave the
> prayse that he came home to
> end his dayes and whilst in my
> grave to sleepe I praye the
> lord my soule to keepe
> Watter Iones deceased the
> 14th day of February 1656

Neglectful decay and wartime destruction overtook
the castles of Gwent with few exceptions, and though
some were used as defence during the Civil War, it was
after Glyndwr had destroyed much of their structure.
Some, such as Cas Troggy, had probably fallen into
disuse earlier, and did not come into the later Border
troubles. But Raglan Castle is the one exception, being
built in the fifteenth century, and it must have been a

beautiful building, with its workmanship less crude than in the fortresses of earlier days. Here was both defence and home, and it was thought unlikely, I dare say, when the castle was built, that such a disturbance as the Civil War would destroy its splendour.

The contemporary account of Thomas Churchyard is more revealing than any historical research. The interest lies in the fact that whereas most of Gwent's castles were already ruined in his day (a fact he very much laments), Raglan was standing in all its glory.

> Not farre from thence, a famous castle fine,
> That Raggland hight, stands moted almost round:
> Made of freestone, upright as straight as line,
> Whole workmanship, in beautie doth abound.
> The curious knots, wrought all with edged toole,
> The stately tower, that looks ore pond and poole:
> The fountain trim, that runs both day and night,
> Doth yeeld in showe, a rare and noble sight.

Churchyard's marginal note says: "The Earle of Worcesters house and castle. The Earle of Penbroke, that was created Earle by King Edward IV buylt the castell of Raggland sumptuously at the first."

Now that was in 1587, and the sight of Raglan delighted Churchyard, who took his enjoyment readily if his long poem is a fair indication. The poem is "The Worthiness of Wales, a Poem. A true note of The Auncient Castles, famous Monuments, goodly Rivers, faire Bridges, fine Townes, and courteous People that I have seen in the noble Countrie of WALES, and now set forth by THOMAS CHURCHYARD". A great deal of the verse is devoted to a section called "A Description of MONMOUTHSHIRE", and Churchyard annotated the verses with references to the owners of the various stately homes he mentioned in the poem. The dedication to "the Queene's most excellent Majestie, Elizabeth", and the gift of the verses "to every loving and friendly reader" completes the beneficence of the author, an eager chronicler of his time, although the Reverend Coxe called his work, in a rather superior manner, "quaint versifications".

Raglan Castle was first built in the twelfth century by the de Clares, lords of Usk and Chepstow, but it was not until the fifteenth century that the castle took its later form, being built by Sir William ap Thomas (a son of the Llansantfraed manor and of the Wern-ddu Herbert heritage, of which more later), who died in 1446. He married a daughter of David Gam, and with his father-in-law, and the Vaughan family of Tretower, he opposed Owain Glyndwr at every opportunity. The effigies of William ap Thomas and his wife are among the many effigies in Abergavenny church. Their son took the name of Herbert from a Norman ancestor, and was, therefore, the first of that name, a family living throughout northern Gwent. The titles came thick and fast on the family at Raglan, and this son of William ap Thomas became the first Earl of Pembroke. His grandson became Earl of Huntingdon. The Earl of Huntingdon died in 1491, leaving a daughter who married Sir Charles Somerset, who was in direct (though illegitimate) descent from John of Gaunt, thus creating the Somerset line, Lords of Raglan and Earls of Worcester. The fifth Earl of Worcester was created Marquis in the first year or two of the sixteen-forties.

The Somersets were always very loyal to the Crown, and it is interesting that the present Lord and Lady

Raglan live at Cefn Tilla Court, which was the headquarters of the Ironside, Fairfax, during the siege of
Raglan in the Civil War. Raglan was the last stronghold
to fall, the siege lasting from June 1646 to the 19th
August, when the defenders were unable to hold it any
longer. King Charles stayed at the castle several times
during the war.

The Marquis was not a young man at the time of the
Civil War, and soon after the surrender he died, a
prisoner, his estates confiscated and much of his wealth
gone in providing financial assistance for the Royalist
cause. His son, Edward Somerset, Lord Herbert, later
Earl of Glamorgan, gave financial help, and did a tremendous amount of work in gathering together Royalist
regiments and working for the King in many ways.

At the raising of the siege of Raglan, the castle was
destroyed, leaving among the fairly extensive ruins
"Y twr melyn Gwent", the yellow tower of Gwent,
hexagonal in shape and surrounded by a moat. The
income of the estate was forfeited until 1660: the timber
had been sold and the possessions dispersed. The estates
were restored on the accession of Charles II, but the
debt owed to the Worcesters by the Crown was never
repaid; though in 1682 Henry Somerset was made Duke
of Beaufort, inheriting Badminton, which became the
principal seat of the Beauforts. The Beaufort Arms here
and there in Gwent—at Tintern, Chepstow, Monmouth,
and Raglan itself, among others—commemorate the
name. I understand a number of cottages in the vicinity of
Raglan are patched with pieces of castle stone, in some
cases a whole staircase having been used. But it is a
scheduled ancient monument now, and such infiltrations have ceased.

That son of the Marquis of Worcester who helped his father in the Royalist cause was famous for his numerous and very varied inventions, many of which were well before the times, but the war interrupted his endless pursuits, as wars have always interrupted the pursuit of peace and happiness by people whose loyalties have conflicted with their peaceful desires. After the war he published a book, *A century of the Names and Scantlings of such Inventions as at present I can call to mind to have been Tried and Perfected which (my former Notes being lost) I have, at the instance of a powerful Friend, endeavoured now in the Year 1655 to set these down. . . .*

One of these inventions was a forerunner of the steam engine, and in Raglan church there is a little notice marking the occasion of a recent visit of an engineering society to pay respect to this early engineer.

The church at Raglan had been so much destroyed by Cromwell's forces at the time of the siege that little of historical interest remains. The few effigies remaining of the Somersets, many of whom were buried in the vaults, were hopelessly ruined, and it is difficult to form any impression of them. Two of the windows are rather unusual. One was given by friends of the Duke of Beaufort on the occasion of his son's marriage in 1872. This window is made up of various coats of arms, and makes a bold, colourful display for a happy occasion. Among the heraldic designs are those of John of Gaunt, the Herbert arms, and those of the first Marquis of Worcester. The other window which is unusual is the one dedicated to the first Lord Raglan, a soldier of many campaigns, by forty-five sergeants of the Army who had fought under this Field Marshal.

I have written that the paternal home of Sir William

ap Thomas of Raglan was Llansantfraed, and in the tiny church there is a large stone inscribed with the names of many of the family, beginning with Thomas ap Gwillim ap Jenkin, father of Sir William. Thomas married Maud, the daughter of Sir John Morley of Llansantfraed.

NERE THIS PLACE LY ENTERRED THESE DEAD BODIES
UNDERNAMED

THOMAS : G L M : IENK : ESQ 8° IUL : 1438 & MAUD
HIS WIFE DAU TO SR : IOHN MORLEY KNIGHT & HIS
COHE : PHIL : THERE SONE & HEIRE 9° : NO : 1460
& IOHAN HIS WIFE, DA & HEIRE OF THO : BLETHIN
OF PENTRE, ESQ 7° : IUN : 1458 : DAVID THERE SONE
& HEIRE 19° : DE : 1510 : KATHE : HIS WIFE DA : TO
SR : ROGER VAHAN KNIGHT 26 : MAR : 1520 : THOM :
THERE SONE & HEIRE 3° : APR : 1537 : 8
IANE HIS WIFE : DA : TO IOHN THO OF TRE OWEN ESQ :
13° : AUG : 1533 : IOHN THERE SONE AND HEIRE 30° :
MAII : 1553 : BUT GWEN HIS WIFE DA : TO EDWA :
IONES OF ABERGA : GEN : WAS BURIED IN HER BROTHER
EDWARS SEPULCHER ON THE NORTHE SIDE OF THE
HIGHE ALTER IN SAINT MARIES THERE : 23 : SEP : 1597 :
WATER THEIRE SONE AND HEIRE 17° : AP : 1606 AND
LETTIS HIS WIFE DA : OF IOHN WILLMS, OF NEWPO :
GEN : 19° IAN ; 1623

Beneath this inscription, which almost amounts to a genealogical table, is another block of writing:

FOR AN ETERNAL TOKEN OF RESPECT
TO YOU MY SIRES, THESE STONES I DOE ERECT;
YOUR WORTHY BONES DESERV OF ME IN BRASS;
A RARER TOMBE THEN STATELY HATTON HAS:
BUT SITHE MY MENES NO PART OF SUCH AFOORDS
INSTEDE THEREOF ACCEPT THIS TOME OF WORDS.

144

Horse-shoe Bend, River Wye, and Wyndcliffe

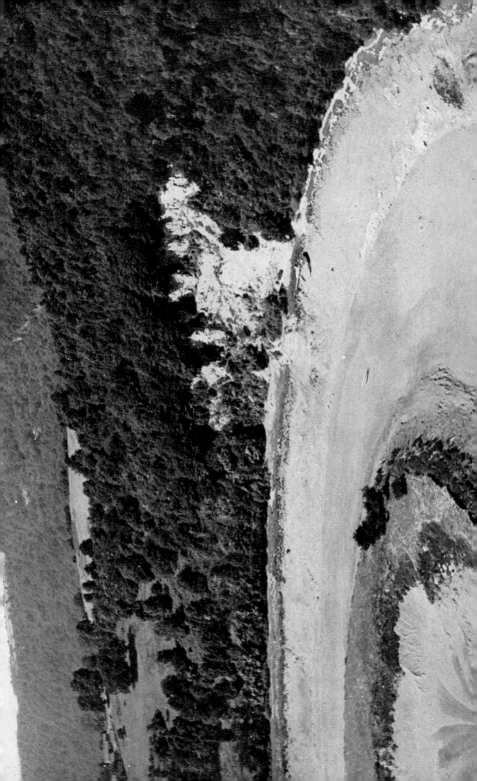

The stone was erected in 1624 by a descendant, and the long link with these early Herberts (for they were descended from that early Herbert ancestor in the reign of Henry I) is continued today. Another memorial in the church records the end of four hundred years of the lineal descent of the proprietors of Llansantfraed Court, from the early fourteen-hundreds to 1804.

Llansantfraed Court is now a country club, and the little church, with its open door and simple flowers on the altar, is only to be found by going up the drive to the house, and there it stands, amid trees. Above the altar are two small alabaster panels in relief, of the Crucifixion. By the style of the soldiers' armour, and the onlookers in the other panel, these would appear to be very early work indeed, and are quite remarkable.

In a county of castles it is almost surprising to find a castle that is a castle only by name and was built in 1790. Yet that is Clytha Castle, built on a hill among trees, and in a lovely part of the country. The ornate battlements need no comparison with the rugged age of the fortresses of Gwent. Clytha was built as a token of remembrance of his wife by William Jones (of Clytha House, with its "Gothic" gateway, *circa* 1790, below the castle). The inscription tells the story:

This building was erected in the year 1790, by
William Jones of Clytha House, Esq.,
Fourth Son of John Jones,
of Lanarth Court, Monmouthshire, Esq., and
Husband to Elizabeth, the last surviving Child
of Sir William Morgan of Tredegar, K.B.,
and Grand-daughter of The most noble William,
Second Duke of Devonshire.

Wye Valley

It was undertaken for the purpose of relieving a Mind
Sincerely afflicted, by the Loss of a most excellent Wife;
Whose Remains were deposited
in Lanarth Church Yard, A.D., 1787,
and to the Memory of whose Virtues
This Tablet is dedicated.

Elizabeth Jones was eulogised to an even greater extent
upon the memorial in Llanarth church. This memorial
goes to great length, and I shall quote only in part:

Her Goodness and her Worth
were so eminently conspicuous,
that the most finished monumental eulogy
would vainly endeavour to display them.
Yet as she always modestly shrunk from observation,
and studiously strove to conceal her various
Endowments;
Justice to her Memory requires,
that some, tho' a very imperfect, sketch
of her Character be here attempted:
She was blest with every hereditary Virtue
of the most illustrious House of Cavendish:
meek, humble, patient,
generous, friendly, noble;
Happily adorn'd with a most extensive Genius,
her Knowledge was vast and uncommon:
In Poetry, Music, Botany, and all the polite Arts,
She excell'd;
as her Manuscripts abundantly testify:
To enumerate her Virtues were impossible;
She was, in short,
Purity and Innocence itself:

for if ever those Virtues were personified,
they were in her.
An utter Stranger to every species of Detraction,
She never spoke of her neighbour, but with praise and
commendation.
With a Heart ever bleeding at the Distresses of others,
the great business and delight of her Life was
"To do good, and to distribute."
Being too good to continue any longer in this World.

You might remember that "this best of wives" was the
daughter to that Sir William Morgan of Tredegar whose
character was praised on the memorial in Lower Machen
church.

Clytha House itself, though of old foundation, was
rebuilt in the eighteenth century. The entrance known
as the Perthir Gate to Clytha House was taken from an
ancient Herbert residence near Rockfield, where a
branch of the family known as Powell lived from about
the fourteenth century to 1715. In 1545 Reynold ap
Howel of Perthir was Sheriff of the county, and this is
where the ap Howel no doubt became Powell. For many
years Clytha has been in the family of Llanarth Herberts,
known by the name of Jones from the sixteenth century
until, in 1848, the old family name was taken as being
more fitting for the senior existing branch of the ancient
heritage. The name Jones arose from the son of John ap
Thomas (a Herbert of Treowen) being named William
ap John, John becoming Jones and being retained as a
surname.

Two of the largest estates in the county were joined
when the Llanover heiress married Arthur Jones of
Llanarth in 1846. The Llanarth estates would be the old

Herbert lands, mainly agricultural, while the Llanover estates included land around Abercarn and the industrial districts. It was this Arthur Jones who, two years after his marriage, took on the old name of Herbert. The Herberts, by whatever name, have, in the main, remained true to the old religion, and in the grounds of Llanarth House is a Catholic chapel.

This part of the county is very much linked by its family connections, and I hope they are not becoming too muddling in this incomplete form.

The early families of Llanover were the Prichards, the Rumseys, and the Cecils, until, in 1792, Benjamin Waddington, not a Monmouthshire man, purchased Ty Uchaf, a property at Llanover. The present Llanover House was completed in 1836. His daughter, Augusta, married Benjamin Hall, who inherited industrial property in the county, including the valuable Abercarn estate, from his father, who had married Charlotte Crawshay. As we have already seen in previous chapters, Richard Crawshay of Cyfarthfa presented his son-in-law with several industrial properties.

Benjamin Hall, the younger, in politics a Whig, was appointed Chief Commissioner of Works, and as such was responsible (and enthusiastic) for the erection of the clock tower of the Houses of Parliament. Several times the bell cracked, but always Sir Benjamin spoke in its favour and supported the architects. When a name was being sought for the clock, a Member jokingly suggested "Big Ben" in honour of its champion, and "Big Ben" it was. In 1859 Sir Benjamin became the first Baron Llanover.

Lord Llanover was obviously an enthusiast, but his wife (who survived him by many years), the daughter of Benjamin Waddington, was, in a more local manner, an even greater upholder of her own ideas. Augusta, Lady Llanover, though English by birth, carried on her own Welsh revival. Naturally, Llanover itself saw most of her efforts, and each house and cottage still bears its Welsh name, including The Gwesty, the little Temperance House, for no inns were allowed too near Llanover. Folk music was revived, and musicians lived at the big house: the Welsh harp was played, and even today an old lady lives in a cottage at Llanover who was a famous harpist. Lady Llanover's bardic name was Gwenynen Gwent, the Bee of Gwent. As far as Gwenynen Gwent was concerned, there would have been no question, as there has been of recent years, of whether the Eisteddfod should be held in Welsh or English. She might have been English by birth, and a hybrid Monmouthshire woman by adoption, but her sympathies were Welsh to the extreme, which is much more than can be said of most Monmouthshire folk today, who, like myself, have divided loyalties between England and Wales.

Apart from her ardent efforts to encourage the old Welsh culture, Lady Llanover was also an authoress, an accomplishment in the nineteenth century when domesticity was an art in itself without need of further embellishment. She was the editress of the letters of Mrs Delany (Mary Granville), with their world of literary London, of Swift, Samuel Johnson, and Mrs Thrale. Mrs Delany was a family connection, and from her Lady Llanover inherited the ten volumes known as *Flora Delanica*. This collection was a series of paper cut-outs of flowers in minute detail, and carried out by Mrs Delany in what she called "paper mosaick". The botanical accuracy is apparently amazing, and the whole collection was left by Lady Llanover to the British Museum.

The Llanarth and Llanover estates became one when Lord and Lady Llanover's daughter, another Augusta, married Arthur Jones of Llanarth, and (as I have already written, but I repeat it to avoid confusion!) two years later the reversion to the name of Herbert took place.

Llanover is a place to explore. There are the Welsh names on the cottages; there are the puzzling letters and dates on the old buildings, including the early Congregational Chapel; there are the church by the secluded river, and the delight of the countryside. The architecture is good, and much that is old and beautiful remains. The farm, which is now known as Cwrt y porth hir (or court of the long entrance), and was once the old Llanover Court, lies back off the main road, with its sixteenth-century look unchanged. The great entrance door proclaims its name.

The new village, too, does not detract from well-ordered Llanover. This is a stone-built village designed by Alfred Powell on the instigation of Lord Treowen (Ifor John Caradoc Herbert), the grandson of Lord and Lady Llanover.

Outside the old post-office, where the stream runs swiftly past neat, colourful gardens, is an old picture, of some unknown date, of the Mari Llwyd. The Mari Llwyd was a Christmas custom performed in many villages at the festive season. A small party of young men went to various houses, knocked upon the door, and the ritual began. One of the young men wore a white horse's head mask upon his own head, and he would sing a rhyme to the people inside the house. These would answer, also in rhyme, and so the evening went on, with some sort of forfeit if those inside the houses failed to reply in verse, and a certain amount of merrymaking when Mari Llwyd and the attendant spirits were invited to share the Christmas cheer. The origin of the Mari Llwyd is uncertain, but it is an ancient custom which has now died out. I believe impromptu verse-speaking is still an art in parts of Wales, but not in Gwent as far as I know. This all points to an inherent quickness for a rhyme, which is akin to music, and comes from a long poetic tradition, even though the Mari Llwyd took a rough form of execution.

The river at Llanover, and, indeed, from Abergavenny to Usk, is a lovely thing, unless it is roused by storms. Here is fishing, and a limpid coolness. It is difficult to describe the peaceful quality of the whole stretch of country on both sides of the river, and each person must find his own pleasure in the fishing, the green meadows, the shadowy Blorenge, or the blue distant Sugar Loaf and Skirrid Mountains. For those who are tired of walking up hill and down hill, here is more gentle land, hedge-bordered lanes, the parkland of the big houses (rarely, alas, occupied), and old cottages of some charm.

I have already mentioned the old forge at Estarvarney in connection with the monks of Tintern, and later the Hanbury family. This eventually was heard of no more, but in the early nineteenth century there was a forge on the other side of the river, at Trostrey, now back to its rural remoteness. Charcoal was used in the forges until coal production came into its own, and it is likely that the Trostrey forge closed up as the manufacturing of iron took its place in the coal-mining valleys. The iron from Trostrey was sent to Newbridge-on-Usk by road, and from Newbridge it was shipped to Newport on the river. Today the placid river at Newbridge belies this early activity.

Close to Trostrey, its church sharing the same rector,

is Bettws Newydd, one of those places, like Llangwm, which you have to find, because it does not stand on the main road for all to see. The church was built by Aeddan ap Gwaethfoed, lord of Clytha and Grosmont, about the same time as Clytha and Bryngwyn churches which he also founded. Clytha church fell down a long time ago. The porch of Bettws Newydd is full of Youth Club notices and other signs of a full parish life, and the whole place shines a welcome. Restoration is obvious, but fitting, with newly pointed rough stone walls and pseudo-antique lighting. The ceiling of this little building is of brown and white panelling, and the carpet is blue, and there, as a beautiful framework to the altar, is the magnificent rood screen and loft in black oak. This is a perfect thing, with stone steps on the south side leading to the gallery, where a big cross surmounts the back wall. This carving is of the fifteenth century, and is one of the few complete screens in the county. In his description of Bettws Newydd the Reverend Coxe shows himself at his most superior: "It is, however, worthy of particular observation, as the ancient rood-loft is entire, and a large wooden cross is still affixed at its eastern extremity; the carved work of the gallery is not inelegant." Not inelegant, indeed. It is beautiful.

This is lovely country. It is the dairy-farming land where the grass grows rich on the red sandstone soil. The farms are mostly large, and carry on mixed farming, with dairying to the fore. The river is made for fishing, and the land for farming. It is comfortable country. And the mountains make a fitting background. Comfortable though it may be, the Usk turns brown and wild on occasion, and floods the surrounding countryside.

Tucked away down a little lane, all on its own, is the

Tintern Abbey
Tintern Parva, Wye Valley

little church of St Mary the Virgin, at Llanfair Kilgeddin. Though this is an ancient church, it has been restored, leaving a certain number of notable features, including a little medieval glass and the ancient tomb of a priest, indicated by its symbolic incisions. But there is something in the church one would not expect to find in this soft green land: the colour of warmer lands in the Sgraffito work which covers the walls.

This work is only to be found in not more than half a dozen other churches in the whole of the United Kingdom, and is an Italian form of art, though in the case of Kilgeddin it was executed by an English artist, Heywood Summer, in the eighteen-eighties, and was in memory of Mrs Lindsay, the wife of the Rector of the parish from 1872 to 1912 (he was also Rural Dean of Raglan). To complete the work the walls were first laid with clay, and the pictures or decorations incised in the clay while it was still wet, and the colouring laid on, then glazed. But that is very briefly what happened, for there were many processes before the work became the colourful completed pictures. The theme of the Benedicite was used by Heywood Summer at Kilgeddin, and some of the pictures have a local background and a rural simplicity, while others are more symbolic.

In the hidden lanes around Kilgeddin are snowdrops, of great size and purity.

The name Kilgeddin has recently been taken far afield in a rather different connection. Lieutenant-Colonel Harry Llewellyn lives not far from Llanfair Kilgeddin, and he is in the British Show Jumping Team, and competes in various International Horse Shows, bringing home the honours, including, this year (1950), for the second time, the King George V Cup from White

Standing Stones, Trellech
Drybridge Street, Overmonnow

City. Perhaps Foxhunter, that popular horse, is more well-known than Kilgeddin, but Kilgeddin's name takes a bit of Monmouthshire with him when he competes in the International rings. In this year's King George V event Colonel Llewellyn took the prize with Foxhunter, and third place with Kilgeddin.

Towards the end of the summer the place is full of every kind of agricultural show imaginable. The posters go up, sometimes for little local shows, sometimes the big ones at Abergavenny, the Bedwellty, or the Monmouth Show.

Certain people one is bound to meet at these events—they are always gathered together at all the country affairs, the ploughing matches, hedging and ditching, sheepdog trials, gymkhanas, hunter trials, and all the rest. The veterinary surgeons, the hay and straw dealers, the farmers, all thoroughly at home. The townsfolk come by car or 'bus; most of them are the town-dwellers who would be happier living in the country, and so do all they can to spend their leisure emulating their country neighbours. It is something to do with this general mix-up of country and industry in Gwent. As I have said before, it is never very far to find a bit of country, or a pleasant stretch of fishing. These town-dwellers even look personifications of all we expect a countryman to be: yellow ties figured with foxes' heads or horses' heads are worn, with hacking jackets and squashed felts. These country-lovers mingle with the county families, the farmers, and the little men in breeches whose very gait emphasises the close affinity between groom and horse. At some of the gymkhanas, especially the ones near the towns, there is a tendency for some of the riders to have met a horse for the first time socially too recently in life, but then there are the times when the horse and rider seem to think as one, and instinct does the rest.

There is something very satisfying about agricultural shows generally, an air of pleasure and the pleasant seriousness of a good job well done. The language is the same whether the people are partaking of refreshment from either side of the big marquee (thick tea out of thick cups, or warm beer served over a wet trestle table), or sitting having a picnic meal on the running-board of a car.

There is no lack of little churches in the Vale of Usk, and in another tiny lane on the other side of the road, but not far from Kilgeddin, is the church of Llanvihangel Gobion (or Llanvihangel-nigh-Usk). In full Welsh this would be Llanvihangel Duffryn Wysg, but I have never heard it called that. Yet again, this tiny place is given a Roman bias, with its occasional name of Llanvihangel-juxta-Usk. This church is past the most unorthodox post-office of all, and that is quite a feat in a county of rural post-offices, and it is built right on the banks of the Usk, in the secluded shade of trees.

In the churchyard is an early-Victorian double tomb-stone, bearing the names of two elderly people, and having a thankful epitaph upon it for the lady, and a rather more urgent one for the gentleman, one David Harry:

> Sick and sore long time I bore
> Physicians strove in vain
> Untill God alone did hear my moan
> And eased me of my pain.

Then the warning to sinners:

> A sudden change by death was gave
> That I no longer time could have
> Believe in Christ make no delay
> For sudden Death do call away.

To the left of the church porch on the exterior wall is a most unusual small stone tablet, with figures carved in relief. The carving depicts two men, presumably in priests' habit, and between them is something which looks to me like a large heart.

A little nearer to Abergavenny is Coldbrook House, which belonged to the Herberts from the middle of the fifteenth century until the early eighteenth century. It was the home at one time of Sir Richard Herbert, a brave soldier who fought under the White Rose in the Wars of the Roses.

Coldbrook was purchased by Major Hanbury of Pontypool for his son Charles. At Caerleon we came across the charitable bequests of Charles Williams, who left the bulk of his fortune to this son of his friend, John Hanbury. Charles Hanbury became Charles Hanbury-Williams, and a country estate was also one of the conditions of inheritance. Coldbrook was thus purchased.

Charles Hanbury-Williams became Member of Parliament on the death of his father, in the days of Fox and Walpole, and he was knighted in 1746, but he will be best remembered for his verses. He wrote political satire, witty observations of his day, and privately circulated verses liable to cause trouble whenever they were brought to the notice of the people concerned. He addressed poems to the fair sex, and seemed to love all the ladies concerned. He had periods of insanity, and died at the age of fifty, in 1759.

In 1891 Coldbrook went back to the Herberts when it was purchased by Lady Llanover. The house she purchased was mostly eighteenth-century, and not the original fifteenth-century home of the Herberts. There are various stories connected with the house, including a secret passage to Abergavenny Castle, and a blood-stained oak floor, but the ghost in this case was only visible to the Hanbury-Williams family.

Abergavenny is a busy town, but it lacks as a whole the character of Chepstow, Monmouth, and Usk; but all market towns, to me, have a fascination. What it lacks in charm is more than compensated for by the wonderful surrounding country. The Sugar Loaf and the Skirrid always seem to belong to Abergavenny. The Skirrid is known, too, as the Holy Mountain, for it is said that on the happening of Calvary the great mountain was rent in twain. Then along the road from Raglan the country is delightful.

The town was Roman Gobannium, and is at the confluence of the little Gavenny River with the Usk.

The castle saw an appalling amount of bloodshed before its destruction by Owain Glyndwr in 1403, when he burnt the town. The castle was built by Hamelyn de Balun, first lord of Abergavenny, and conqueror of upper Gwent, of which Abergavenny was the main town. Hamelyn also founded the Benedictine Priory of Abergavenny.

Some three miles south of Abergavenny, near Penpergwm, was Castell Arnallt, an ancient fortress, said to be the home at one time of Arnallt (or Ernallt), son of the giant, Bwch. In the twelfth century it was the stronghold of a Welsh prince, Siesyllt (sometimes known as Sitsyllt), who considered himself to be among the many descended from King Ynyr. The relationship between the natives and the Normans must have been very touchy, for what happened at Abergavenny was duplicated throughout the Border lands, in lesser degree, for at least two hundred years.

Siesyllt killed Henry, uncle of William de Braose, and lord of Abergavenny, but the incident was, to all intents, ignored. William de Braose followed his uncle as lord of Abergavenny, and an invitation was extended to Siesyllt and many of his knights to attend a great feast at Abergavenny Castle, with de Braose acting as genial host. This gives an indication that it was not unusual for there to be amity between the Normans and the Welsh.

Inside the banqueting hall the visitors, about seventy in all, were overcome by de Braose's men, and massacred without a chance to retaliate. The real horror of this story was added when William de Braose sent out his men to Castell Arnallt, knowing that the lord and protector, Siesyllt, together with his men, was lying dead at Abergavenny. Cadwaladr, Siesyllt's little son, was murdered while his mother watched helpless, and then she too was killed.

About seven years later the Welsh took certain revenge for this slaughter, but the completeness of the cruelty of William de Braose was never forgotten. This "eye for an eye" revenge kept the Border troubles always ready to break out, for one generation would repay an injury suffered by a previous one, and kinsmen would remember a hurt incurred by another.

Within the lofty beauty of the Priory Church at Abergavenny are several records of local history. There are so many effigies in the church that the effect is almost uncanny. These effigies form a record, though incomplete, of the lords of Abergavenny, and of other notable families in the district. One of the earliest effigies is that of Eva de Braose who died in 1246. She was the daughter of William Marshal, Earl of Pembroke, and wife of William de Braose, lord of Abergavenny and grandson of the

William de Braose who murdered Siesyllt and his followers. This William de Braose was hanged for leading a lady into the ways of infidelity. This lady was Joan, wife of Llywelyn the Great, and a warrior of his calibre was unlikely to allow such a thing—especially when a Norman was involved.

Another early tomb is of Christian, the lord of Llanllowell's wife, who between them began the Herbert race. More will be heard of Christian when we reach her childhood home, Wern-ddu.

Sir Richard Herbert, of Coldbrook, and his wife, Margaret, lie silently together. Sir Richard died in 1459, an unpeaceful end to his soldier's life, for he was beheaded after the battle of Banbury. His namesake, Sir Richard Herbert, this time of Ewyas, who died in 1510, occupies a place under a canopy.

Sir William ap Thomas of Raglan Castle, and his wife, David Gam's daughter, Gwladys, are two more representatives of the Herberts.

Several other monuments are of doubtful origin: one might be of Lawrence de Hastings, thirteenth lord of Abergavenny; another might be a Cantelupe or a Nevill, both families having held the lordship. The eleventh lord, John de Hastings, is represented by a wooden effigy of the early fourteenth century.

Apart from these more notable figures there are others of men (and their wives) whose lives were sufficiently important to allow their images to remain for posterity. And there is the huge Jesse tree of the fifteenth century.

In the chapels where the effigies of Abergavenny lie, there is the beginning of local history. These might seem like inanimate carvings, but to work back to their comparatively short ancestry, and to trace their contemporary

159

pattern and subsequent families, would be to visit many old Monmouthshire houses, to unearth records of simple domesticity and historical turbulence, romance and battle, the shaping of our heritage. At Abergavenny this is noticeable by the very quantity of monuments, but each church has, behind the impersonal stones, a human story or historical background, and anyone wishing to trace a county's history could begin in a less favourable place than an old church.

CHAPTER V

WENTWOOD

". . . I ascended to the summit of the eminence called the
Pencamawr, a high point of the elevated ridge which stretches
from the Treleg Hills through the midland district of Monmouthshire and terminates near Caerleon. On reaching the
height, a glorious prospect suddenly burst upon my view. From
the midst of the forest scenery I looked down on the rich vales of
Monmouthshire, watered by the limpid and winding Usk,
dotted with numerous towns and villages, and bounded to the
west by the long chain of hills which stretch from Pontypool,
and terminate in the mass of mountains above Abergavenny. In
this variegated landscape I caught the first glimpse of the Sugar
Loaf and Skyrrid, which from their height and contrast form
the principal features in the prospects of this delightful country.
. . . The road is a narrow level way, leading through groves of
coppice, interspersed with oak, beech, and other timber trees."
—William Coxe, from *A Historical Tour through Monmouthshire*,
1801.

FROM Ridgeway and other parts of Newport there is a
dark hill in the distance, and that is Wentwood. As you
walk along the Bulmoore road from Caerleon you are cut
off on the one side by steep fields and scrubland, and
towards Newbridge there are trees and also places where
trees have been hewn, and that is Wentwood too. From
the main Caerleon to Usk road the view is more panorama-
like, and when the sun shines to make the slopes golden,
then Wentwood is beautiful. For most of the journey
from Newport to Chepstow the various escarpments of
Wentwood rise and fall, but there are fertile fields leading
to the woods. Then there are the two hills, Mynydd
Allt-tir-fach (called Mynydd Turvey, or Money Turvey),
and Grey Hill (Mynydd Llwyd in Welsh, but more often

called by its English name). These are known as the
twin peaks of Wentwood, and one or other, or both, are
often seen, from parts of the moors, from part of the
lovely Usk to Chepstow road—suddenly the twin peaks
are there.

And that is today, when Wentwood has become smaller,
and is connected more with daffodil fields, a reservoir
where trout can be caught, and forestry plantations than
anything else. Even today it is a landmark. At one time
the great forest of Wentwood divided the cantref: north
of it was Gwent Uchcoed, and south of it was Gwent
Iscoed, above the wood and below the wood. An early
eighteenth-century record says: "The Forest or Chase of
Wentwood extends itself on the rising Ground thro' the
Middle of Upper Gwent, from the River Wye to Uske,
being about 8 miles in Length, and 4 in Breadth." This
must have included the Chepstow Park Wood to extend
Wentwood to the Wye, which geographically is easily
associated with Wentwood. The meadows on the two
hillsides were, in the eighteenth century, worth twenty
shillings an acre. Money is such a difficult comparison,
for at twenty shillings an acre that land was valuable
indeed.

The most fertile land in Gwent was once south of the
great forest, and one part of it was famous throughout
Wales as the most wonderful wheat land, with innumerable bees. This was Maesgwenith, the wheat fields, on the
banks of the Troggy Brook just above Llanfair Discoed.
The name begins in legend, but continued until probably
the sixteenth or seventeenth century, and there was a
house of the same name. The Kemeys family were its
owners at certain times. The name seems to have died out
now. Although legend began the story, there is no

doubt that Maesgwenith was, in fact, a fertile stretch of land, and is so now.

The story of the fertility of Maesgwenith is part of an old Welsh story told in the Triads (where everything was grouped in threes). Coll, a swineherd, was in charge of a sow, Dallwaran, in some part of the British Isles, and Dallwaran was a wanderer. She burrowed her way to the coast and then became seaborne. Wherever his charge went, Coll clung to her bristles. Dallwaran eventually landed at the mouth of the stream which begins its life in Wentwood. In her mouth she carried three grains of wheat and three bees, and these she dropped on the banks of the Troggy, and from that time onwards the wheat and bees flourished until Maesgwenith's fame was spread throughout the land. Strangely enough, the very first time I can remember seeing anyone in a complete bee-keeper's outfit was in a garden on the fringe of Wentwood, not so far, as a bee flies, from Maesgwenith.

Of the six Agrarian Castles of Wentwood, four are still in various stages of existence. The six were Cas Troggy, Llanfair Discoed, Penhow, Pencoed, Dinham, and Llanvaches, but today Dinham and Llanvaches must come away from the list as far as seeing any ruin is concerned. The history of these castles is never particularly clear, but it is generally supposed that they were built in the reign of Henry III for the defence of the Royal Chase, though sometimes on the site or foundation of an older building; and Cas Troggy and Llanfair are on the way to becoming like Dinham and Llanvaches, having become deserted when their primary use was over. Penhow and Pencoed eventually became farms, and more of the original structure was preserved, incorporated in the later dwellings. The six castles are always linked together as the six Agrarian Castles of Wentwood, yet their histories do not always appear to coincide. One thing they do have in common, and that is the fact that they do not seem to have figured in the important Border risings.

Pencoed Castle seems a long way from Wentwood today, yet its name is "top of the wood" (Pen-y-coed, as it is often written), and it was one of the places entitled to "house-boot" and "hay-boot" from ancient times. This castle has had several phases of life, and there are records of a Sir Richard de la More living in the place in 1290 and possibly much earlier. It was built in Henry III's time, but in 1483 the building took a more permanent shape, or at least the building was begun and went on into the early sixteenth century. If Sir Thomas Morgan (a cousin of the Tredegar Morgans) had not taken over the castle in 1483 it would, I expect, have suffered the fate of Llanvaches and Dinham, as by that time the need for defence was slackening, and the castle was not being used as an outpost of Wentwood.

As you walk along the road from Llandevaud, Pencoed is suddenly there between a break in the hedge, with its great gatehouse. In the church of Llanmartin, the village below Pencoed, is Sir Thomas Morgan's tomb, with all his children, girls on one side and boys on the other. This is a stone monument, the figures in relief, and rather an unusual and good example of early sixteenth-century work. Sir Thomas, who fought at Bosworth, and whose descendants were great fighters, died in 1510.

Pencoed became linked in the fifteenth century with Penhow, not only by virtue of both coming within the forest's laws, but also by the marriage of a daughter of Sir Thomas Morgan to Sir Thomas Bowles of Penhow. This Sir Thomas Bowles descended on the female side from the first owners of Penhow, the Seymours. The early part of the castle, including the tower, was built by Sir William de Sancto Mauro in the twelfth century, possibly on the site of an even earlier building owned by the same family, while in the thirteenth century more work was added (perhaps this was by order of Henry III, but this castle was definitely already in existence before his reign), while by the fifteenth century the castle was probably completed. The name of Seymour was a corruption of St Maur, in Normandy, from where the first of this Norman family came and took their name. Below Wentwood's slopes there is a piece of land still called Parc Seymour.

When Sir William de Sancto Mauro was building Penhow, it is likely the local inhabitants were hostile towards the Norman invader who was taking up permanent residence among them, but in time the family must have become part of the cycle of country life. When the direct male line came to an end, a daughter inherited the estates, and the Thomas Bowles who married a Welsh Morgan's daughter was of that line, a generation or so later. In 1674 the estate was added, by purchase, to that of Lewis, of St Pierre. There could not have been much land near the coast, within quite a distance of St Pierre, that did not belong, in one century or another, to the St Pierre family.

The purely domestic residence of Penhow was built after the restoration of Charles II, and the warm-coloured buildings, set as they are on a little hill, are a perfect picture of swords into ploughshares. The castle is part of the farmhouse now, and the church, in the same warm stone, with its low, conical-hatted tower, is immediately behind. The church is probably as old as the castle.

Although Dinham Castle is no more, it seems that as early as 1128 a building of some sort was in existence, while in the Wentwood Survey of 1270, Adam de Dinam was given as the proprietor of the manor. Later, a family called Welsh or Walsh took over the manor of Dinham until 1569. However, all this is not particularly concrete, and even less concrete, but possibly of some help in the tracing of Dinham's history, is a supposed translation or transcription of the Lays of Caruth, a bard who lived at Dinham Castle. There is something unauthentic about these Lays, which sing of defeating the Romans, and of the burial of Caractacus at what must be the great Iron Age fort at Llanmelin. But for what little truth the Lays might contain about Dinham (completely overcome by modern wartime infiltration), I will quote part of "Lay the First":

"The castle of Dinham is mighty to view, it lieth to the north of the great city; its batteries what foe can encounter? the warriors from afar waged war with Llewellin: with men of might he strove, but the spirit of peace was with Llewellin, and his vassals subdued them. I sing thy glories, O Dinham! The moat which encloses thy castle is fearful to view; the stranger vieweth thy turrets and wondereth at thy strength."

The "great city" is Caerwent. The bard was more accurate than prophetic when he sang "that the unborn shall pass over the ruins without heed".

William Blethin, born at Shirenewton Hall in the sixteenth century, purchased the manor of Dinham for his children. He was Bishop of Llandaff, and considered himself to be descended paternally from Howell Dda, and therefore of Royal Welsh blood. The Blethin family lived at Dinham thereafter. A Timothy Blethyn of Dinham was the father of Temperance, who married into the family of Lord, of Kemeys, and died in 1805, aged eighty-nine. She was buried in little Kemeys church.

Cas Troggy is on the northern fringe of the woods as the road rises from the Usk, and before it disappears into the plantations which make up much of present-day Wentwood. Unlike most of Gwent's castles, it does not appear to be very strategically well placed, as it lies in a field rather lower than any of the surrounding country: the first impression is that it was built in a hollow. It takes its name from Trogi, a giant, son of that giant Bwch who lived beneath Mynydd Maen, and brother of all those other big fellows around Usk, so whether the thirteenth-century castle was built on the foundations of a much earlier castle built by Trogi, I do not know; but there again, Trogi's castle would have been some sort of fortified mound, I should imagine. It has been thought that the castle was built by Roger Bigod, lord of Chepstow at that time, and that it became the residence of the Ranger of the Forest. Old records have it that the castle was known as Striguil. At some unspecified time I have read of an Earl of Trogi who wooed the maid of Dinham, with disastrous results to himself, as he was already betrothed to another.

The place is thoroughly neglected now, and by history. Enough remains to form an impression of Gothic architecture in the three large arches which are well preserved, overlooking the moat. The whole of the outside foundations can be traced, but the ruins have now deteriorated into a cattle shelter.

In the field next to the castle a spring bubbles up through the boggy grass, and becomes the Cas Troggy

Brook, a long stream which runs around the edge of the woods, then right down past Caerwent. Here it changes its name to the Nedern, until it runs into the Severn at Caldicot Pill, where it was likely that the Romans landed.

Like Cas Troggy, the castle at Llanfair has become a shelter for animals, this time pigs, but the styes are not in the main part of the ruins, which stand on the lower slopes of Wentwood.

The manor of Llanfair Discoed was purchased by his parents for Rhys Kemeys, and in 1635 the manor house, now a farm, in the centre of the village, was built by Rhys. On the opposite side of the road, but probably once belonging to the manor house, is one of the few remaining old pigeon-houses in the county.

The name of the village means St Mary's Church under the Wood, and there it is, the little church hidden below the great ivy-covered wall of the castle. The church was rebuilt in 1865, but in the porch is an old stone which was removed from its duty as a stile in the churchyard. On the stone is incised, quite roughly, but deep and clear:

> Who Ever hear on Sonday
> Will Practis Playing At Ball
> it May Be before Monday
> The Devil Will have you All.

Although not dated, this stone must have some connection with the *Book of Sports* which caused the first breaking away from the Church, and the origin of Nonconformism.

James I originated the instructions contained in the *Book of Sports*, but it was in 1633, when the Royal Command came again, that the feelings of a certain section of the clergy rose to great resentment. Part of the

Rolls Hall, Agincourt Square, Monmouth ; with Rolls and Henry V monuments
The Skirrid

Royal Command contained in the *Book of Sports* instructed that:

"As for our good people's recreation, our pleasure is that after the end of Divine Service, our good people be not disturbed, letted, or discouraged from any lawful recreation, such as Dancing, either man or woman, Archery for men, leaping, vaulting or any such harmless recreation, or from having Maypoles, Whitson Ales, or Morris dances, and the setting-up of Maypoles and other Sports there with used."

These words had to be read from the pulpits of all churches, and those clergymen not complying with the order were ejected from the living. At this time the rector of Llanvaches was William Wroth, and he refused to read words which, to him, were not only distasteful but seemed to strike at the very heart of religion as he practised it. The whole trend of the Church was disturbing to a man of Wroth's integrity, and he found many who followed him in his way of thought. In 1639 he opened the first Nonconformist house of worship in Wales, at Llanvaches, and such was his power as a preacher that the congregations overflowed beyond the doors of the building. The present building at Llanvaches bears no trace of the original. His successor was Walter Cradock of Llangwm, a famous preacher and writer, and one who must have learned much from the sincerity of William Wroth.

Puritans were much in evidence in Monmouthshire in the seventeenth century, and the lower slopes of Wentwood were often the scenes of religious persecution. In 1658, at Shirenewton, two women, Elizabeth Holme and Alice Birkett, were found holding a meeting in the name

169

Black Mountains from Campston Hill
Grosmont Castle

of the Quakers in the house of Walter Watkins. There was a great commotion, and the two women were taken before the justices and subsequently imprisoned. This kind of thing was taking place all over the country in varying degrees of seriousness, but there is no doubt that Nonconformism generally was taking a great hold in the county, rising to its peak in the nineteenth century with the growth of industrialism.

Of the same district and religious convictions as William Wroth was Wroth Rogers, a famous Parliamentary soldier, and likely, by his name, to be a kinsman. His son, Nathan Rogers, was a fighter too—a lawyer, and so a fighter with words. In 1708 he published his *Memoirs of Monmouth-Shire, Anciently call'd* GWENT, *and by the Saxons,* GWENTLAND. This, beginning as a potted history of the county, goes on to appeal against enclosure of part of the Forest of Wentwood in 1678 by the Earl of Worcester, of Raglan Castle. The appeal is directed to the Earl's grandson, the then Duke of Beaufort, for "a voluntary and just Restitution of what his Grandfather wrested from the Tenants of Wentwood".

In 1215 the Charter of the Forests granted by King John to his subjects laid down certain laws for the protection of the contents of the Crown Forests, and also laid down privileges, as well as laws of punishment, for the tenants. In the Charter was a section dealing with the Swainmotes (or courts), where offenders were fairly tried at given intervals:

"And furthermore, every forty days throughout the year, the Verderers and Foresters shall meet to view the attachment of the Forest, as well of Vert, as Venison, by Presentment of the Foresters themselves; and they who committed the offences, shall be forced to appear before them."

Other sections of the Charter dealt with privileges:

"Every Freeman for the future may erect a Mill in his own Wood, or upon his own land, which he hath in the Forest; or make a Warren, or Pond, or Marl-pit, or Ditch, or turn it into Arable, without the Covert in the Arable Land, so as it be not to the detriment of his Neighbour."

Every freeman could also

"have in his Woods the Ayries of Hawks, of Spar-Hawks, Falcons, Eagles, and Herons; and they shall have likewise the Honey which shall be found in their woods."

Apart from being almost poetical, these were very definite rights to which the tenants of the Royal Forests were entitled.

These laws must have been in existence for Went-wood, which was a Forest of the Crown, although it was not until 1270 that the Survey of Wentwood was made, listing those who could have houseboot (the right to cut timber for house-building) and hayboot (the right to cut brushwood for fences), and besides the more obvious residents of Wentwood, such as those of Llanfair, Langstone, Redwick (well down on the moors), Pencoed, Penhow, Dinham, Crick, and Llanvaches, these included that Abbot of Tintern, the Prior of Striguil, and the Prior of Kinmark. (Striguil was Chepstow, and Kinmark a priory of ancient date near Piercefield.)

The laws of the forest which were carried out by the tenants and the officials had conducted forest life quite successfully, and at the Foresters' Oaks, now only a name, Privy Sessions were held, the various cases were heard, fines paid, and problems solved. Then after centuries of comparatively smooth running, in 1678, Henry, Earl of Worcester, enclosed part of the forest, cut down trees, and generally disturbed the smooth flow of the foresters' lives. The Earl was acting, so he said, under the terms of a grant by Charles I, but the foresters were under the impression that no grant had ever been given. Certainly, the Worcesters lost a tremendous amount of money in the Civil War, which was never repaid at the Restoration, but the confiscated estates were handed back, probably, however, without any additions.

Nathan Rogers' publication was, as much as anything, an exhortation to the Wentwood residents to awaken from their lethargy and demand their rights: "He can't be of a true British Heroick Soul, that bows his Neck so easily to the Yoke of Slavery." Perhaps Nathan Rogers' main arguments are worth quoting too, which he addressed:

To the
Right Honourable the Earl of Wharton, Guardian to
    Sir Charles Kemys Baronet
Sir Hopton William Baronet
John Morgan Sen and John Morgan Jun of Tredegar
    Esqs
John Jefferies of Pencoyd Castle ⎫
Tho. Lewis of St Peere |
William Gore of Langston |
George Kemys of Kemys   ⎬ Esqs
William Blethin of Dinham |
Edward Kemys of Pertholy   ⎭

Tracy Catchmead of Crick ⎱ Esqs
John Walter of Peircefield ⎰

Edmund Bray Esq; and the other Heir of Sir Edward
 Morgan

Richard Lyster of Moyns-Court ⎱
Charles Jones of Magor ⎪
George Howel of Penhow-Castle ⎬ Esqs
Thomas Price of Lanfoist ⎪
— Fielding of Little Tinterne ⎰

The Provst, Fellows and Governour of Eaton-Colledge,
 and the other Gentlemen and Tenants of Wentwood

I have quoted those names in full, as some of the old
family names recur there (what a delightful name is Tracy
Catchmead), and here again is the Eton College connection with this part of the county. The Earl's infiltrations
disturbed the lowly and the rich, all those whose lives
were bounded by the forest laws. Nathan Rogers sternly
challenged the landowners in particular, as no doubt
their protestations would carry more weight:

"You are Gentlemen that have considerable Estates
and Interests in the County of Monmouth, within the
Verge and Purlues of the Forrest or Chase of Wentwood, or adjacent thereunto; your Ancestors, You,
your Tenants, and other particular Persons from times
Immemorial, have had Right of Common, or Estovers,
Pannage, House-Boot and Hay-Boot (as they call it) as
well as the cutting and carrying away all sorts of Wood
and Timber, without stint or Limitation, for the use of
those Mansion-Houses and Tenements, Anciently
free within the Liberties of the said Chase, which was
without interruption always enjoyed until Henry Earl
of Worcester, of Ragland Castle, by some Grant, or

173

pretended Grant, from the Crown, did in the Time of King Charles I enclose or cause to be enclosed for his own use, by his Tenants and Vassals, to whom was Demised great part of the old Chase; who are now become in Elections a dead Weight on the Freeholders. But the late Duke of Beaufort his Grandson, in the latter end of the Reign of King Charles II, being Lord Lieutenant of the County of Monmouth, Governour of Chepstow Castle, and Lord President of all Wales, with an Army of Workmen and Soldiers, Vi and Armis, enter'd into the Residue of the said Chase, who were employ'd, some for felling, cutting, cording, and coaling the Wood; others to make Walls, Fences and Mounds to enclose the said Chase, and the Soldiers keeping a Guard there to protect those Tumultous Assemblies of Rioters (which were so found at a Quarter Session at Monmouth) wholly intending to exclude the Tenants and Commoners of their Ancient and Undoubted Rights and Privileges, which our Roman and British Ancestors preserv'd, and left to us inviolable."

(Pannage is the right to turn swine into the forest, and estover the right to cut timber for repairs.)

A fresh edition of Nathan Rogers' *Memoirs* was published, in 1826, by S. Etheridge, of High Street, Newport, and this edition is prefaced by a venomous attack by the editor. This pamphlet seems to have been reissued on the occasion of more infringement upon the rights of the Wentwood tenants, but the editor's preface is less subtle than Nathan Rogers' lawful questioning, and strikes at individuals of the Beaufort family. This seems to be a forerunner of modern politics, with plenty of mudslinging, and lists of emoluments earned by the Beauforts as Government servants, adding to the one, "and as much as his conscience will allow besides", which is rather hitting below the belt. Samuel Etheridge was a Chartist, a colleague of John Frost, and his printing presses must have had many hot words through them.

Nathan Rogers himself had the rights of a forester, as he lived within the Chase. In 1658, when the laws of the forest were moving smoothly, he was Foreman of the Jury of a Speech-Court held beneath the Foresters' Oaks. With several others, including Edward and John Kemeys, Thomas Blethin, and Nathaniel Field, gentlemen, and Philip Edwards and Meredith Howel, yeomen, he was taken to London for trial in 1678, when the trouble of the enclosure began. Sir Nicholas Kemeys was, at that time, the Ranger of Wentwood.

The estimated loss of privileges, in money as distinct from the loss of traditional rights, amounted to about £300 a year. Here is that connection with Eton College again, for the name was included among the tenants' losses: "Aeton College of Goldclift and 100 acres, £20." Others bore a greater loss, up to about £80, when one tenant had more than one estate, as in the case of the Morgans and Kemeys:

"Sir Charles Kemeys, Baronet, for his privilege and freedom of House-boot and Hey-boot in the said Chase, for his Mansion-house at Lanvair, and six Tenements there, and for the Priory-house and Vallice Farm in Caldicot, computed to be worth per annum, £50."

You will have noticed the repetition of the family name of Kemeys. In order to place it, roughly, I will say that

Kemeys Inferior is close to Caer Licyn, the ancient tumulus. On the top of the hill is Kemeys Folly, directly below that, towards the River Usk, is Kemeys House, and below that again, in a hollow by the river, is the little church of Kemeys. This family left its name to two places in Gwent, for Kemeys Commander, in that lovely country of the Usk Valley near Trostrey and Bettws Newydd, was the home of the first Kemeys to come to Britain. That first Kemeys was a Norman who came with Hamelyn, conqueror of Gwent, and settled beside the River Usk, and whose descendants moved down to the seclusion of the lower reaches of the same river. On the banks of the Rhymney were other houses belonging to the family. Later, in the struggle for the rights of the Wentwood tenants, it is interesting to see that the native Morgans and Norman Kemeys are as one in their defence of privilege.

Elizabethan Kemeys House remained in the senior line until about 1700, while Bertholey House, burned down some years ago, was also a Kemeys residence. Bertholey is near Newbridge, where the green slopes of Wentwood rise to the woods. In 1593, Edward Kemeys of Bertholey was Member of Parliament for the county, and in 1601 he became Sheriff.

Then there was the family at Llanfair Discoed. Already we have seen Rhys (what would his Norman ancestors have thought of *that* name!) building the manor-house there in 1635, and in 1678 poor Sir Charles lost £50 in privileges for the mansion-house and his other properties.

After the Kemeys of Kemeys Inferior came the Lords, whose memorials are in the tiny Norman church. Now the old house is a farm, its great chimneys proclaiming its age. Although the Lords were not a local family, and

Grosmont Church

bought Kemeys about 1700, by 1719 Lawrence Lord was Sheriff of the county. In 1699 George Kemeys had been Sheriff, the last of many of the family who had held office since 1566, though I believe some part of the family lived in Newport after the eighteenth century.

Above Bertholey, in the woods, are what are known as the ruins of Will of Wentwood's house. All I have ever been able to find out about Will was from an old countryman, who told me "he was a proper rascal".

Perhaps I am wrong to include Christchurch in this chapter. I know today that it is almost part of Newport, but that is only because Newport has spread its suburbs into the old country districts. Then it is often linked with Caerleon, but it stands too high above the river to come within the Usk Valley. To me, Christchurch has always been one with the ridge of high land of which Wentwood is part, for along the Roman road is Catsash, and then the woods.

To write of Christchurch itself is a sad experience. When I began this book the old church stood in ancient glory, a well-loved church, seen on its hillside from all around, with its Healing Stone, its playfully named "Beauty" (a stone carved with a grotesque face), its Norman work, and the very love itself with which Christchurch has always been regarded.

Then one night, the 5th November, 1949, the church was burned down, a horrible bonfire night indeed. In time of war churches were bombed, and sorrow was felt, but this happened for no apparent reason. Guy Fawkes' Night celebrations were blamed, yet there was a feeling that this was no accident. People of all denominations and no denomination at all were shocked and saddened.

On the following Saturday night St John's Church,

Skenfrith Castle

Maindee, went up in quick flames, leaving one of the largest parishes in Newport with only a shell of a church. The whole town, and county too, were stunned by this second blow. Two gaunt ruins have to be rebuilt (partly from the widely drawn public donations) because of the destruction caused by a warped mind. Some news, local or national, affects one section of the public, and another incident affects someone else, but the burning of the churches cast an unnatural tension over the whole town: I have never known anything quite like it. However far we are going away today from things spiritual, there is, I am sure, a deep-rooted feeling which is still there to be stirred.

Christchurch, on its hilltop, will rise again from its bare walls and tower, which is intact, but much that is old and beautiful has gone for ever, save in memory. Christchurch has always been a kind of symbol, seen from so many places high on its hill.

Wentwood is a grand place. It is good to walk where the Llwynau Brook runs, and the secret lanes spill their flowers and spread their hedges high. Then from the top you can see the Usk below where it winds from the north to Caerleon, twisting all the way. On the other side, the Chepstow road side, you can look right across Newport, where the Usk widens and flows into the Channel. All the way along the Chepstow road there are lanes leading to Wentwood, through hilly fields before the woods close in, and there is Earlswood Common with its bracken and the little roads running at the side of the woods.

Most of the woods are plantations now, but there is still a certain amount of mixed woodland. Through the plantations are dark tunnels, and the ground is soft with larch needles. Great nests of wood ants, made from the dry

178

needles, surround some of the trees, and the whole place smells of the trees. But the plantations are only part of Wentwood. Some of it is parkland, some bracken-covered moorland, with the twin peaks, Mynydd Turvey and Grey Hill with its stone circle and the bracken golden in the sun.

CHAPTER VI

THE WYE VALLEY

"The Wind-Cliff comprehends all the scenes of the Paradise, in what is called a prospect: the winding river with all its singular accompaniments; the farm on the peninsula; the waving woods, in numerous forms, contrasted with the bare and ragged rocks; the town, the castle, and the bridge of Chepstow; the whole surrounding district, which, though in common form, appears ornamented, where every hilloc is happily placed, and presents some circumstance interesting to the eye; the splendid course of the Severn, here called a sea; and the hills of Glocester and Somerset, forming a magnificent section of the horizon; compose a prospect which in variety, beauty, and grandeur, the author has never seen surpassed."—David Williams, from *A History of Monmouthshire.* (1796.)

WHAT more beautiful boundary to any county could there be than the River Wye, with Chepstow at its gateway?

The importance of Chepstow, once a fortified town, as a port and shipbuilding yard has diminished, although the yards still produce dock-gates and small craft, and during the last war turned out landing-craft. During the 1914–18 war ships were completed at Chepstow, and I have been told that this was the only place where ships were launched ready to go to sea, fully equipped. As far back as recorded history Chepstow has been a port and shipbuilding centre (the river is tidal as far as Llandogo, with a very high spring tide). In the eighteenth century, in his Chepstow poem, the Reverend Edward Davies, rector of Portskewett (and later of Sudbrook), wrote:

> Corn, cider, timber are exported hence,
> And ships are built, for traffic and defence:
> The Irish trade increases ev'ry day,
> And ships from Chepstow visit Dublin Bay.

Chepstow still smacks of its shipping days around The Back, with its tall, ramshackle warehouses, old cottages, and the derelict Boat Tavern.

The centre of the bridge over the Wye at Chepstow marks the boundary between Gloucestershire and Monmouthshire.

In the centre of the town is the old Town Gate with its narrow span across the hilly main street. Up goes the street out of the town, and down it goes, twisting to Beaufort Square, and turning narrowly and even steeper to the river. Edward Davies again:

> But, strange to tell, there cannot here be found
> One single inch of horizontal ground.

It is still like that, much of it still old, with that pleasant mixture of history, agricultural implements, hay and corn merchants, dozens of little pubs, and a few bigger hotels that have the appearance of having been there for a very long time, of being part of the picture of a market town. I like Chepstow.

Castell Gwent, or Cas Gwent, is the Welsh name of Chepstow, which comes from the Saxon Chepe stow, or market town. The town probably began to flourish in the seventh or eighth century, when Caerwent, the once important town of southern Gwent, fell into decay. Leland, the sixteenth-century writer of *The Itinerary of Wales* had this to say:

> "A great lykelyhood ys that when Caerguent began to decay then began Chepstow to florish. For yt stondeth far better as apon Wy there ebbyng and flowying by the rage cummyng owt of Severn. So that to Chepstow may cum greate shippes."

The Norman conqueror of this part of Gwent was William Fitz Osborne, and he began to build the castle with its Norman keep, a fortress in a magnificent position above the Wye, with a history as turbulent as any castle in Monmouthshire. About 1074 Gilbert de Clare became the lord of Chepstow, and the family of de Clare held it for some time, founding the priory church and Tintern Abbey. Already there had been a priory at Chepstow for some centuries. This was Kinmark, which must have fallen into decay a couple of hundred years ago. The Prior of Kinmark was entitled to house-boot and hay-boot from Wentwood (Chapter V).

After the de Clares came the inevitable changing of ownership of the castle, which was growing to formidable strength. There were the Marshals and the Bigods (both through marriage to heiresses to the estates); the estates were surrendered to the Crown, and came into possession of Thomas de Brotherton, son of Edward I and brother of Edward II, and in the fifteenth century the Earls of Pembroke added Chepstow to their many possessions in Gwent.

This family were still owners of the castle at the Civil War, and several battles were fought for possession, with both sides in turn successful. The Parliamentary forces took it from the Worcesters, and it was regained from them by Sir Nicholas Kemeys with the help of that turncoat Sir Trevor Williams, who at that particular time was fighting for the Royalist cause. Later, Cromwell's soldiers routed the castle, killing Sir Nicholas Kemeys in the fighting.

One of those who was a judge at Charles I's trial, and signed the death warrant, was Henry Marten. At the Restoration the regicide was imprisoned at Chepstow

Castle, where he died some twenty years later, after a
comparatively comfortable imprisonment, living in what
is now known as Henry Marten's Tower of the castle,
with his wife, and visiting, among other places, St
Pierre Park.

Henry Marten was buried in Chepstow church, and
wrote his own epitaph, using his name as the first letter
of each line:

Here or elsewhere (all's one to you and me)
Earth, fire or water gripes my ghostless dust
None knows how soon to be by fire set free
Reader if you an oft try'd rule will trust,
You'll gladly do and suffer what you must,

My time was spent in serving you, and you
And death's my pay, it seems, and welcome too;
Revenge destroying but itself while I
To birds of prey leave my old cage and fly,
Examples preach to the eye—care then (mine says)
Not how you end, but how you spend your days.

Beneath a large canopy in the church is the tomb of
Henry, second Earl of Worcester, and Lord Herbert of
Chepstow, Raglan, and Gower, who died in 1549 aged
fifty-three years, and his wife Elizabeth. It is as well that
they were buried at Chepstow and not Raglan, or there
would be no tomb to see after the destruction by Cromwell's army. There is no doubt that these effigies would
have suffered the same fate as the other Herbert memorials
at Raglan. There is still a faint colour about the tomb,
and it must have been very bright in its original state.

The most colourful tomb in the part-Norman church
is "In Memory of Thos. Shipman and Margaret his wife
(Daughter of John Maddock of Wollastone, Gent) and

their 12 children. Also Richd. Clayton Esqr who was married to Margaret the Relict of the above mentioned Thos. Shipman, 1620". This communal tomb shows the twice-married Margaret lying full-length beneath the canopy and behind her are the two husbands, very similar in appearance, both kneeling before little lecterns, holding open Bibles. The base of the tomb is taken up with the twelve children of Thomas and Margaret. On the left are two sons kneeling, and on the right ten daughters, two large ones, and eight smaller ones behind them, all bundled together. The interior walls of the canopy are painted black, and one side bears a painted skeleton. This is indeed a riotous-looking tomb, with the colours of black and red predominating.

Up the hill and out of Chepstow town is Mounton, a tiny, dreamy village. To me it will always be "the deserted village", because the first time I went there, one autumn, that is how it appeared. The rain was pouring down, the lanes were deserted, and not a soul stirred. And now I find that it is usually quiet, but not with a sad quietness, just a tucked-away peacefulness. In fact, it is a bright place, with flowered gardens and a neat, restored church in the hollow. What give an illusion of desertion are the ruins. These are the ruins of old mills, once run by the pretty Mounton Brook, and now no more. The population of Mounton has never been very great, so many of the mill-workers must have lived in Chepstow. Paper was made at Mounton, including notes for the Bank of England, and also carpets and cloth, exported from Chepstow. The names of the mills echoed the gentle countryside, Lark Mill, Lady Mill, and Linnet Mill. As early as 1567 Lady Mill was in operation, and some were in existence, I believe, until the nineteenth century. Though to see

Mounton today is hardly to warrant such industry. At various places along the Mounton Brook, in the early nineteenth century, were six paper mills, and also four corn mills.

There are two roads from Chepstow to Monmouth, one being the main road alongside the Wye, and the other, reckoned as part of the Wye Valley, but used much less than the other, away from the river, and, to my mind, one of the most lovely roads to travel in the county.

The road through Trellech begins quietly enough, going through the Chepstow Park Wood, and not far away, on another road through Chepstow Park Wood, is Itton Court, a fifteenth-century home of John ap Gwilym (an early Herbert), and later belonging, through marriage, to the Morgans of Pencoed, and taken over by John Curre of nearby Rogerston Grange in 1790. The present house is of relatively recent date. Sir Edward Curre, a well-known local figure, died about twenty years ago, but Lady Curre still continues with the famous pack of white hounds, in existence for well over a hundred years. These hounds have rough coats, and "Lady Curre's white hounds", as they are known, give a good day's hunting through the wooded country of the Wye and thereabouts. The hounds have Welsh and English strains in them, including the Llangibby strain, which has a long history.

For all who remember Captain Fox as M.F.H. the lines written by Raglan Somerset "In Memoriam" are a touching tribute to a man killed in the recent war:

Somewhere far off he lies,
Twixt the torn pavé and the bomb scarred field
Of Flanders, he was one who dies
But does not yield

And him no tocsin sound of hound or horn
Can rouse on this November morn.
Yet when the Autumn hedgerows burn
With fires of dying red and gold,
Surely his spirit will return
To those dear coverts, loved of old,
The slopes of Coed-y-ffern,
The Gockett and the kindly gloom
Of Wern-y-Cwm.
There under Newchurch hounds shall be
Down to Cae-Pwta running free,
Until 'neath soft November skies
The White Hounds music fades and dies
Amid the bracken of Ty-vree.

Through Chepstow Park Wood the road begins to climb, and as it climbs the country all around comes into sight until it culminates in the splendour seen from the highest part of the road. Somewhere above Devauden the country opens up, with higher wooded land towards the Wye, and the spaciousness of mountains and plain across the county. Between Trellech and Monmouth, before the road goes downhill, there are views which must be hard to equal anywhere. I daresay that is a sweeping statement, but the whole thing—the colour, the ranges of hills, the plain between, and the moorland where you are standing —is magnificent.

This is generally known as the Wye Valley, although it is away from the Wye, and I would choose it against the main Chepstow–Tintern–Monmouth road. I hope that is not upsetting too many theories, but that is my opinion.

In 1543 a Walter ap Robert of Pant-glas (green

hollow), between Llanishen and Trellech, was Sheriff of
Monmouthshire, and again in 1555. In 1636 a Henry
Probert of Pant-glas is listed as being Sheriff (he married
Ann, daughter of Giles Morgan of Pencrug on the lower
reaches of the Usk). This is a good example of the derivation of a surname. The ap Robert was eventually merged,
becoming Probert. Many of the Welsh surnames have
been derived in that way, besides the taking of the
father's name as the family name; Pritchard (ap Richard),
Prodger (ap Roger), and no doubt Price was once ap
Rhys, although Prys (Preece) is a truer transcription.
It seems too good to be true that Parry was ap Harry,
but there it is.

There is a record of a grant of privileges to John ap
Howel ap Jenkin of Pant-glas, and either this should read
Jenkin ap Howel, or it is a brother, and I am inclined to
think it must be Jenkin. (His son, Robert ap Jenkin, was
a gentleman usher to Henry VII.) Anyhow, the grant
applied to one of the early Proberts, the ancient family of
Pant-glas, and gives an idea of the rights allowed to certain
people in the wooded lands of the county. The grant, made
in 1436, concerned Wye's Wood (part of the wooded area
of the Wye Valley), and was given by Richard, Duke of
York, Earl of March, from his castle at Usk, "to John
ap Howel and his heirs yearly, two staggs in summer and
two hinds in winter within the aforesaid chase and pur-
lieus of the same, two wild boars, and one shoulder and
the nombles of the same, and of every deer slain within
the said chase". A forfeit of 10*s*. had to be paid for any red
deer killed "more than is before rehearsed". Also, two
broad arrows, ready headed, were to be kept for the Duke
or his heirs should they feel like a day's hunting in Wye's
Wood.

The last Probert (by name) to live at Pant-glas was Trevor, who died in 1680. The family then lived at the Argoed. Later, the properties were divided between two daughters, and eventually (in 1814) came into the possession by descent of Colonel Morgan-Clifford. The old farm of Pant-glas lies just off the main road.

In Trellech church is a sundial, once kept somewhere in the village, and this was given in 1689 by Lady Magdalen Probert (widow of Sir George Probert and daughter of Sir Charles Williams of Llangibby), to perpetuate the various unusual features of the village, once, apparently, a town of some importance.

Trellech means the stone town, and is named from its three Neolithic stones, misnamed "Harold's Stones" after a supposed victory in battle between the Welsh and the Saxons, but, in fact, of a much earlier date. The stones have been given various explanations, but it does seem that they were used in some Druidical rites. The photograph in this book gives an excellent idea of their formation. On one side of Lady Probert's sundial is a picture of the stones, with the measurements on each one—8 ft., 10 ft., 14 ft.

Another side of the sundial depicts the tumulus of Trellech, which was probably the site of a Norman motte and bailey. There is a story that anyone attempting to excavate the mound would bring calamity upon themselves, but that might have been one way of keeping any intruders away from the stronghold in more superstitious days.

The third side of the sundial shows the Virtuous Well, once known for its healing powers, but now neglected in its field near the source of the Olway Brook.

So although Trellech is a quiet village, surrounded by

farms and with its two inns, much history, often of an
obscure nature, I admit, once livened the heights of
the lovely country. It is likely that the township of Trellech never recovered from the battles between the English
and Glyndwr's forces in 1404, at the same time as the
battle at Craig-y-Dorth, beyond Trellech, when the
English suffered defeat.

But it is the church which completes Trellech's feeling
of the past. And surely such a lofty church was not built
for a small village. The early fourteenth-century builders,
building on an earlier site, were erecting a church of some
size and importance, unless they really felt the glory
of God as they built the pointed, high arches and gave
those spacious lines. Until very recently the walls were
coloured pink, and I thought the colour became them
well. They are now washed in the more usual cream
colour. There are more memorials to the Rumsey family
than any other, which is understandable, as they lived at
Trellech Court from the sixteenth century to 1846, and
some of them lived at Wolvesnewton. Even earlier than
the Rumseys were the Seymours and the Catchmays
(also of Bigsweir and Monmouth), until the Rumseys
took such firm possession for about three hundred
years.

The pulpit in the church was once a seventeenth-
century three-decker, and the beautiful plain dark oak
high altar rails are of the same period, about 1640. I am
at a loss to explain the enormous raised tombstone, I
suppose it is, which is at the foot of the 1,400-year-old
preaching cross in the churchyard. It is a solid slab of
stone, on pedestals, and must have some more than
ordinary significance.

Yes, Trellech is one of those satisfying backwaters,.

full of active agriculture and a history that is too much in the atmosphere to be dead.

Between the two roads from Chepstow to Monmouth, the one through Trellech, the other through Tintern, is some lovely country. The road from Trellech to Llandogo begins across moorland, not bleak moors, but abounding with heather, wild flowers, and mountain ash, gay in July and August, with drystone walls bursting with ferns and sprouting grasses and flowers. The air is fresh and full of the sound of birds. The road skirts the wooded Beacon Hill, then as it begins its downward way the woods close in, mostly forestry plantations, with signs of felling and also of new growth. The air is still, and even the birds seem hushed in song.

Above Llandogo the Wye Valley itself opens out, and when I see the mixed woods up-river and on the opposite banks in great green billows, I wonder why I often say the Wye Valley scenery is overrated. And in the autumn the whole splendour of the Wye Valley has a last colourful fling before the winter.

From the valley it is a pretty sight to see the little houses in the protective trees of the steep cliffs above Llandogo. The Wye Valley villages have the charm of most riverside villages. The inn known as The Sloop gives a reminder of the old shipping days when Llandogo was a harbour.

Once a year, for a few days and nights in the spring, along the Wye, in particular at the weirs around Llandogo, elvers are caught in numbers too enormous to be known. As they move along the river the tiny eels are caught at the weirs, a squirming mass of uncountable creatures. I understand 9-cwt. was a recent record for one man's one-night catch.

Wye salmon is famous. "A Chepstow salmon's worth his weight in gold", in fact, and one was netted at the beginning of this half-century at $63\frac{1}{4}$ lb. at Llandogo. The lower reaches are not so good for trout, but the salmon make up for the deficiency.

Part of the steep woods above Tintern is known as Barbadoes Hill, and I am sure this must be connected with Lewis Morris, who had an estate in the district. He was a Parliamentary soldier, and on the Restoration found it prudent to leave the country, and it was to Barbados he went. The journey was a profitable one, as he and his brother Richard, who went to America (Lewis joined him in time), became wealthy and of some importance in the New World. It was a member of the same family, Colonel Valentine Morris, who acquired Piercefield Park in 1736 and lived beyond his means, and whose charity extended beyond his financial capabilities. Piercefield is now the Chepstow racecourse (where Gordon Richards rode eleven winners in two days in 1933), and the setting is delightful.

A thing which might appear a paradox in these days of the increasing industrial encroachment is the fact that there is less industry on the banks of the Wye today than there was in the past (I am referring only to the Monmouthshire reaches). The Wye Valley is not the place to connect with industry, yet as early as Elizabethan days there were wire works at Tintern, and there were ironworks until the late nineteenth century, or even at the turn of this century, with the Angidy Brook giving the power for the works. David Tanner, who had the ironworks at Blaendare (near Pontypool), and also at Redbrook, owned the Tintern works in 1775. I think Edward Davies' eighteenth-century description of the works is amazing in comparison with the serenity of Tintern today, where the only industry (if that is its true name) of any note is that connected with tourists:

Black forges smoke, and noisy hammers beat,
Where sooty cyclops, puffing, drink and sweat;
Confront the curling flames, nor back retire,
But live, like salamanders, in the fire;
For, at each stroke that's by the hammer giv'n,
From the red iron fiery sparks are driv'n,
In all directions round the forge they fly,
Like lightning flash, and quick as lightning die.
Here smelting-furnaces like Etna roar,
And force the latent iron from the ore;
The liquid metal from the furnace runs,
And, caught in moulds of sand, forms pots or guns;
Oft shifts its shape, like Proteus, in the fire—
Huge iron bars here dwindle into wire;
Assume such forms as suit the calls of trade,
Plough-share or broad-sword, pruning-hook or spade:
To all impressions the kind metal yields,
Thimbles for ladies makes, for heroes shields.
These fruits of industry enrich the place,
Where plenty smiles in ev'ry busy face;
The lazy drones are driven from the hive,
For here the active only live and thrive.

Today the life of Tintern is centred around the Abbey, or rather the visitors who include Tintern Abbey in the "Wye Valley tour". I know it is fashionable to decry the more obvious beauty spots, and I admit it is good to find an unknown backwater, particularly for the native who has always been able to see the more well-known places and buildings, but these places of historical and beauteous fame are not popular for no reason—true, they have had

Black Mountains from the Blorenge

the good fortune to have had roads or railways built quite close, but Tintern Abbey, for instance, has enough grace to overshadow the motor coaches standing beneath its walls. Such places were beautiful in the past, or their history made them renowned, and in most cases the original reason for their attraction remains.

To see the glory of the setting chosen by the Cistercians when they built the original abbey in 1131, it is as well to climb to the little church of St Mary's on the Hill (as distinct from St Michael's by the River). The thick rising woods on the opposite bank of the Wye make a dark and solemn background for the ruined arches, and the thirteenth-century builders who enlarged the work of the earlier monks were wise to remain at the same site. The Abbey was founded by one of the de Clares. Some of the work was helped along by Roger Bigod, lord of Chepstow, about 1270. I wonder if those first builders had a vision of the man-made loveliness to come which would join with the splendour of nature so fittingly. As an autumn dusk drifts slowly into night, the Abbey merges with the muted greens and golds above the still river. (For the one who tires of the "hackneyed" scenes—and I have a certain sympathy with him—then why not try an out-of-season visit? Then will the solitude come creeping down and new beauties unfold themselves. All I ask is that the magnificence of scenery and building should not be written down because many other people also want to see things of beauty and delight.)

At the back of the Beaufort Hotel is a rough road which turns into a grass-grown track, rising all the while. It leads between trees which quickly turn into thick, overgrown woods, smelling damply. The woods rise steeply on each side, and the trees meet overhead. Down the one side runs

13   193

Pastoral, Vale of Ewyas

a stream, its banks thick with ferns. It is not what I call a happy wood (except, perhaps, for the fern-collector): there is too much dampness and undergrowth; but it is worth walking through, because suddenly the trees stop, and the lane goes on, still grassy, between hedges at the edge of bracken-covered high land, where the sudden breezes blow. There is farmland here too, with good cattle grazing, and right at the top, by Porth-gaseg Farm, the fields are ploughed and under cultivation, fine rolling land in a patchwork of rich earth, green pasture, and a yellow splash of vetch.

It is a winding, narrow pathway that takes you through the rough woodland to the Wyndcliff. I almost trod on a mole the last time I went there; it moved slowly, but just in time, into the long grass at the edge of the path.

There is a little platform on the Wyndcliff (at the moment marked "Dangerous"), and it makes one feel rather humble to view the largeness of the land, while being such a small thing among the immensity of it all. Most uplands give me a feeling of freedom and vitality, but not the Wyndcliff. The bright green and cultivation of the bulge of land is Lancaut, surrounded by the river in its great horseshoe bend. I have stood on the little Wyndcliff platform in a high wind, and the trees around were in a fury of noise as the branches bent and strained, and there was no room for any other sound. It was rather frightening, because there were so many trees all around, above and below: I looked down on to the roundness of the tree tops, when in full leaf, and they moved in the wind like green waves, flecked with the new gold of September.

There is a lane from St Arvans that goes past Wyndcliff Court to the Wyndcliff, and it is a lane with tall hedges and a profusion of violets in the spring. St Arvans is a nice village, with a new-scrubbed look, and where the cottages lack a front garden, tiny wall gardens have been placed at the foot of the colour-washed walls. It is fitting that in such a neat place a topiarist should carry on his artistry. Here are no large privet peacocks, but miniatures in box. The little hedges in the small garden are trimmed in animal designs, Scottish terriers, jockeys on horses, and ships and swans. And just to round the whole thing off are a pair of wooden cricketers on the line posts, a bowler bowling to a batsman at the other end of the line.

As far as Monmouthshire is concerned, the town of Monmouth is the Wye Valley centre, and a pleasant place it is with its high-spired church of St Mary playing hymn-tunes on its bells on a Sunday morning, and its buttercup fields on the banks of the Monnow more golden than green in May. Agincourt Square, with its Victorian-looking Market Tavern and the usual well-cared-for hotels found in most market towns, is full of activity. The girls from the Monmouth School for Girls cling with white-gloved hands to their wide-brimmed boaters as their bicycles take them down the hill from the Square, and the Monmouth Grammar School boys take their 345-year heritage quite lightly as they finish with their tasks for the day.

Monmouth is a nice old town, with not much of its castle remaining. It was built by Fitz Osborne or Hamelyn, the conquerors of northern Gwent. The Priory was founded about the time of Henry I. Anyone visiting the Wye Valley knows Monmouth, with its old gate-house astride the narrow Monnow Bridge. There is a wide by-pass road being made now to cut off the town for through traffic. As far as I can see, the town is still busy, new road or no new road, and that possibly holds the charm of places like Monmouth: the activity that goes on, and has always been, though the buildings are of the past, mingling with the progress of the years.

Agincourt Square has a life of its own, and the tourists are part of that life but never seem to interfere with the life of Monmouth as a market town. The two monuments in the Square are part and parcel of that life. There is the statue of Charles Stewart Rolls, son of Lord Llangattock of the Hendre, whose name shall for ever be associated with Rolls-Royce, those cars which never lose their look of aristocracy, whatever their age. In his hand he holds a small early-type aeroplane: the Rolls-Royce engine went into the Spitfire, so that all who went through the Battle of Britain can give their thanks to Charles Stewart Rolls, who died in a crash at an early age after a life devoted to the improvement of internal-combustion engines. On the Rolls Hall itself (a Victoria Jubilee commemoration by Lord Llangattock) is that squat monument of Henry V, Monmouth-born, and Monmouth is very proud of her Royal son, and of the bowmen of Gwent who went with him to France.

Through the Monnow Bridge gateway, down the hill, is Overmonnow, once a separate borough from Monmouth, and with the Norman church of St Thomas as its parish church. It does seem distinct from Monmouth even today, with its row of small, old cottages on one side of the church, and on the other side a row of whitewashed, timbered houses, of unusual design. In the more ordinary-type cottages there are a number of bricked-up windows to escape the old tax, and on one of them is moulded a round, moon-like face.

Overmonnow was a centre for cap-making, and known

as the cappers' town. There is a house, once an inn, known as the Monmouth Cap, near Llangua, a long way from Monmouth, where the Monnow flows over the Herefordshire border. These caps were close-fitting, and perhaps the most famous reference to them was in Shakespeare's *Henry V*, when Fluellen said to his king:

"... if your majesty is remembered of it, the Welshmen did goot service in a garden where leeks did grow, wearing leeks in their Monmouth caps; which, your majesty knows, to this hour is an honourable padge of the service; and I do pelieve your majesty takes no scorn to wear the leek upon Saint Tavy's day."

When the Wye and the Monnow become aggravated by storms, there is always a danger of flooding, and about the middle of March 1947, the town of Monmouth, notwithstanding its elevation at some points and distance from the rivers, was severely flooded. Low-lying Overmonnow suffered very badly. The county as a whole was in sad straits, as at one time, about the 21st of the month, the roads leading from Chepstow to Monmouth, Gloucester, and Usk were under water. This inundation was after the great snows of the winter. Six feet was the greatest depth in Monmouth, I believe, and at one time about one-third of the houses in the town had three to four feet of water in them. The havoc left behind, the mud and filth, was indeed dreadful.

A little above Monmouth is Dixton, and the little church of Dixton is on flat land near the river, where the banks are not particularly low. Yet the waters of the Wye rose on the 22nd March, 1947, not only above its banks, but went to a depth of eight feet outside the church, and to six feet within its walls. The scene when the floods receded was desolate, with thick mud on the floor, and every pew and piece of furniture thrown into confusion. Once before, in 1929, the waters had risen to somewhere around five feet.

It must be a constant worry to know that the little church is faced by the relentless rising of the river whenever the storms are fierce or the snows thaw. To go into the church today, without knowing of its struggles, it is difficult to believe that the river has lapped at its walls. The whole place shines with cleanliness: the walls are brightly distempered, and the wood is polished. From the outside the church shines too. It is washed white, and has a stone roof and a little stone spire, and its very whiteness throws out a challenge to the destruction of the river. With its whitewashed walls against the dark green of the woods on the opposite bank of the Wye, it has one of the prettiest approaches to a church that I know, and in the spring it is framed by a tree in blossom.

So there is the Wye, beautiful indeed in its long periods of calm, but a thing of destruction when it cannot hold the water pouring from the thawing snow or falling from the skies in storm.

Vaga, the wanderer, was the name the Romans gave to the Wye.

CHAPTER VII

NORTHERN MONMOUTHSHIRE

"But the picturesque traveller will hardly fail of a lively interest,
while, traversing the superior heights of the neighbouring
mountains, he views the grand extent of the Monmouthshire
wilds, and traces the different combinations of its majestic hills,
which in some parts range into the most sinuous forms, in others
extend for many miles into direct longitudinal ridges; or, when,
withdrawing from the sterile dignity of the high lands, his eye
gratefully reposes on the gentle vallies that sweep beneath their
brows, enlivened by glistening streams, and rich in all the
luxuriance of high cultivation."—J. T. Barber, F.S.A., from
A Tour through South Wales and Monmouthshire (1803).

Two rivers flow into the Wye at Monmouth, the
Monnow and the Trothy, and between them they know
the most beautiful country in the whole of Gwent.
Through the isolated Vale of Ewyas in the Black Mountains flows the Honddu River, and that joins the Monnow
near Pandy. The Grwyne River (a good trout stream)
acts as county boundary in parts.

Perhaps it is because of its comparative isolation that
this northern part of the county is so little known—
'buses every three hours, twice a week, or not at all
during the school holidays, and a train service only on the
fringe, make some districts delightfully quiet and remote.
Its beauty is unforgettable. To me, there is no large
stretch of the county quite like this. It really begins at
Abergavenny on the Brecknock border and makes its
fertile way across the county to the Hereford border. The
Hereford "white-face" cattle have strayed over in quite a
number of places, too, and a little of the Hereford talk.

The churches are border-built, with variations from the more usual square-towered churches of southern Gwent, and the stone is not so grey, but takes the colour of the sun and the soil.

Nowhere is more peaceful than this lovely country, yet it is probably known as much for its three castles as anything:

> Three castles fayre, are in a goodly ground,
> Grosmont is one, on hill it builded was:
> Skenfreth the next, in valley is it found,
> The soyle about, for pleasure there doth passe.
> Whit Castle is, the third of worthie fame,
> The countrey there, doth beare Whit Castles name,
> A stately seat, a loftie princely place,
> Whose beautie gives, the simple soyle some grace.*

Grosmont, Skenfrith, and White Castle are known as the trilateral, or Y Tair Tref, the three towns. Their histories have been linked, at least from the eleventh century. It is thought that White Castle was in existence in the sixth century as a native fortress. At the time of the Norman invasion of Wales three of the sons of Prince Gwaethfoed each held one of these castles.

Gwyn held White Castle, or Castell Gwyn, and it seems there would be no need to look further for the origin of its name (Gwyn means white as well as meaning blessed, fair, or holy). There is a theory that the castle takes its name from its colour, as traces of white have been found on the stones, but I am sure it takes its name from its early owner, the brave Gwyn, who, though old and blind, fought a duel with the Norman invader. The castle was deserted by 1320.

* Churchyard.

White Castle is a *real* castle. I feel as though I should be mounted on an armoured charger as I go across the moat between the two huge round towers. (Or perhaps it would be more appropriate if I said I felt I should be wearing a wimple!)

The moat is now a most peaceful backwater, with a couple of huge carp living there. The swan (whose inadequate name for a swan is Harry) has lost his mate, but has found friendship with a duck. The wild life (though the present occupiers are very docile) causes as much interest as the historical adventures of the castle.

Bach, the eighth son of Gwaethfoed, held Skenfrith at the invasion. The name Skenfrith is a corruption of Ynys Cynfraeth. Ynys means island, and must come from the proximity of the River Monnow, and Cynfraeth was a chieftain in the sixth century. (There appear to be more recorded personalities of the sixth century than any other until Norman times. Ancient records being what they are —and later ones are contradictory enough—it seems that anything pre-Conquest was automatically dated in the sixth century!) In the time of Henry VIII the village was known as Syneffraid. Skenfrith is a very quiet village, and its castle, never of any size, is now crumbling into old age (though work is in course to preserve the ruins), and has apple trees growing in its courtyard. The ruins are of a single tower on a mound, surrounded by the outer walls and battlements.

The church at Skenfrith has a half-timbered tower, and is a fair size for what is now a small village, and it is very ancient. Inside is the monument of John Morgan, Governor of Skenfrith Castle in the sixteenth century, who died in 1557, and of Anne, his wife, who died seven years later. Almost like a museum-piece is the Governor's pew, set aside from the ordinary pews of some more recent date.

Perhaps you remember that the churches of Clytha, Bryngwyn, and Bettws Newydd were founded by Aeddan, lord of Clytha and Grosmont, and it was this sixth son of Gwaethfoed who held Grosmont, while his brothers held Skenfrith and White Castle. I imagine Grosmont to have been the most important of the three, and certainly Grosmont has been, and is, the largest of "the three towns".

The ruins of the three castles are mainly of the period of Henry III. Hamelyn, the conqueror of northern Gwent, first held the castles after the defeat of the Welsh, then the lords of Abergavenny, by name de Braose. In the thirteenth century the castles were granted to Hubert de Burgh, but he lost them, and gained them again from the King in 1232. The early history went the way of many Border castles, with various owners, as the King and barons disagreed. In 1240, however, Hubert de Burgh handed over the three castles to Henry III, who, in 1267, settled the estates upon his son, Edmund Crouchback, Earl of Lancaster. Grosmont became the favoured residence, and was well known as part of the Duchy of Lancaster, and the home, for a time, of John of Gaunt, son of Edward III, who married Blanche, the daughter of Edmund Crouchback. Thus Grosmont was part of the Crown property inherited by Henry IV.

In 1405 Owain Glyndwr's troops burned the town of Grosmont, laid siege to the castle, and Glyndwr was master of the situation for a time until the King sent reinforcements to the castle under the command of his son, young Harry of Monmouth. The Welsh army was

defeated, and the young prince wrote to his father after
the battle:

"My most redoubted and most sovereign lord and
father, I commend myself to your majesty, requesting
your gracious blessing. My most redoubtable and most
sovereign lord and father, I verily pray that God may
show you His miraculous power in all parts.   Praised
be He in all His works: for on Wednesday, the 11th
day of March, your rebels of the parts of Glamorgan,
Morgannwg, Usk, Netherwent, and Overwent, were
assembled to the number of 8,000 people, by their
own account, and went the same Wednesday in the
morning and burnt part of your town at Grosmont
within your lordship of Monmouth. And I at once sent
off my very dear cousin the lord Talbot, and the small
body of mine own household, and with them the
valiant and faithful knights, William Neuport and
Johan Greindre, who were but a small force in all; but
it is well to be seen that the victory is not in the multi-
tude of people, and this was well shown there, but in
the power of God and in the aid of the blessed Trinity,
your people held the field and conquered the said rebels,
and killed of them according to fair account in the field
to the time of their return from the pursuit, some say
eight hundred, some say a thousand, being questioned
upon pain of death. Whether it be the one or the other
I will not contend. And in order to inform you fully of
all that is done, I send you one worthy of credit, my
loyal servant and the bearer of these [dispatches] who
was at the engagement, and did his duty most faith-
fully as he has done on all occasions. And such amend
has God granted to you for the burning of your houses

in the above-mentioned town. And of prisoners there was taken only one, and he was lately a great chieftan among them, and whom I would have sent but that he is not yet able to ride at his ease. And concerning the government which I propose to effect after these [events], may it please your highness to vouchsafe full credit to the bearer of these dispatches in that he will show to your same highness on my part. And I pray to God that he may preserve you always in joy and honour, and grant to me that I may [be able to] solace you speedily with other good news.

Written at Hereford, the said Wednesday in the night.

Your most humble and obedient son,

HENRY."

That letter shows promise of the king that was to be after the wild oats had been sown.

In Grosmont church is a huge, flat-faced stone knight, and this is supposed to be the effigy of one of Edmund Crouchback's descendants. The rear portion of the church today is bare and like an ancient crypt, and is partitioned from the main body of the building. This large structure has five arches on each side, and there are signs of more arches being uncovered from their plaster casings. It is a vast building for the size of present-day Grosmont, and has the importance of an octagonal tower topped by a spire.

The size of the church gives a fair idea of the population Grosmont must have had at one time, though much of this population was composed of the garrison kept at the castle.

Grosmont once had the position of the third largest

town in the county, but this must have faded when the castle fell into disuse. Yet unlike most medieval towns of any size, the importance of Grosmont did not die out with the castle, and the place remained a borough until 1860. The two chief offices in the town were held by the mayor and an ale-taster, and the following year the ale-taster became the mayor, while a new ale-taster was appointed.

It is meet that Grosmont houses a real old craftsman, an ironworker, his work being both useful and good to look upon.

Grosmont always seems to me a little out of this world. It is a delightful place, and I hope it remains rather out of this world, for so few places do. There are no glaringly modern buildings, and most are very old indeed. Then the country around Grosmont is really beautiful, beauty, in this case, surely being in the eye of each beholder.

Because the history of Y Tair Tref is so interwoven I have dotted about the county to write about them together. I have taken the three points of the triangle from Grosmont, which is in the very north, close to the banks of the Monnow, to Skenfrith, also on the Monnow, but towards Monmouth, and then down to Castell Gwyn in the centre. I have gone from one to another without touching the country in between. And what country it is.

There is a little place called Newcastle not far from Skenfrith, set amid quiet lanes where the hedges grow thick, and at first sight it might seem strange that it is called Newcastle, with its few cottages and straight-faced house which was the old school. But the farm on the corner hides part of the old castle, what little is left. The castle was once the fortified residence of a native chieftain, never of any size, but was improved by the Normans and

205

must soon have fallen into decay in the light of so little evidence of existence.

It was known at one time as Castell Meirch, or the castle of the war horses, which lends tremendous vigour and colour to the rolling countryside. The stories that are told in Newcastle speak of fairies—not war horses and knights with pennants flying—and are in keeping with the isolation of the little place. Yet in one room of the old Wellington Inn a justices' court was held periodically, which points to a greater importance than seems apparent today. There is a wishing well down the little lane, and in a field at the back of the inn is the stump of the old New-castle oak, a legendary tree which no one would attempt to fell, or even lop, because of the fairies who had the tree under their power. All who did make an effort to hack the branches away came to an untimely end, or broke their limbs, or had some other misfortune for their folly. Not so many years ago the tree fell down of its own accord, which might have been a case of old age, or that the fairies were tired of their tricks and moved on else-where. Oak trees are said to have a reputation for being connected with fairies and the supernatural.

The inn itself is of uncertain antiquity, and in the spring it has a beauty unexpected even among such beautiful surroundings. It is built as three sides of a square, and might not attract a great deal of notice at any other time of the year, but in the spring, about May, the whole building is hidden in a haze of wistaria, the most wonder-ful wistaria I have ever seen. It is known to be over two hundred years old, and it was not a new plant then. It has a huge trunk on the one wall, and the branches spread right round the three sides until the whole building is covered: the branches are even beginning to creep around the corners and will soon be around the back as well. It is a beautiful, dreamy sight, with the murmur of innumerable bees. . . .

This is the way to go to Skenfrith, through the lanes where so few cars go, passing Hilston Park where you can begin to see the wooded hills of Graig Serrerthin, and up and down the rough lane to drop into Skenfrith itself.

I do not know how other people feel about country 'buses, but I like them. I like the way they stop at all the landmarks, and put down the country women laden with their week's shopping. The conductor throws out a bundle of evening papers, and the passengers welcome one another, and chat, one to another, about familiar topics; they wonder about the absence of an expected passenger, and speak of the ailments of the aged and the growth of the children. I know 'buses which pick up men with rabbits hanging out of bags thrown over their shoulders, and a box with a ferret in it goes up on the rack, and a small, muddy terrier lies on the floor of the 'bus. The country 'bus breaks the isolation of the villages and brings a lonely farm nearer to its neighbours. There is nothing impersonal about a country 'bus, and the longer the journey, the more one is part of the little community jolting about on the often springless seats. The driver nods to his regular passengers, and the conductor asks after a member of the family.

There is a 'bus service between Monmouth and Abergavenny, and it really is a grand trip, tearing through the narrow lanes, overlooking wonderful country with always something to see: rabbits in the fields, a little church spire, magpies, and all the other well-known country sights. The 'bus makes diversions to villages off the main route (Newcastle is one of them), and all this adds to the friendliness and does away with the impersonal atmosphere of most town 'buses.

This road goes alongside Tal y Coed, which was the home of Sir Joseph Bradney, to whom all writers on the county shall be for ever indebted. His large volumes cover practically the whole of Monmouthshire in amazing detail, and were written prior to and after the 1914–18 war. They are the result of what must have been meticulous research, and love for the county too, with the precise genealogical tables, meanings of place-names, ownership of any house of age, and should be seen to be appreciated. Sir Joseph Bradney's ancestors were the Hopkins family of Llanvihangel Ystern Llewern, so his connections came from the heart of Gwent.

It was in one of these quiet lanes, too rough for frequent traffic, that a richly coloured stoat stopped in curiosity, and turned his head a moment, before going into the hedgerow.

Near the Hendre is Parc Grace Dieu, on the Trothy, a farm which was a Cistercian abbey founded in 1229 by John de Monmouth, a nephew of the conqueror of northern Gwent, Hamelyn de Balun. The Welsh, possibly in revenge for the earlier conquest, destroyed the monastery not many years later, though normally the Cistercian Order received better treatment than the Benedictines. In this case, I daresay the monastery was too strongly connected with a successful Norman invader to be tolerated. In many cases it was the Welsh themselves who set up the Cistercian houses.

The lands around the Trothy have many connections with Ynyr Gwent and his son, Iddon, also King of Gwent in the sixth century, apart from the descent of several old families from this royal heritage. Sometimes it seems that all the old families of Gwent can trace their descent to Ynyr.

The lovely name of Llanvihangel Ystern Llewern was given by Ynyr. He lost his way in the darkness of night, and saw a little light ahead of him. He followed the light and became caught in a bog. Unable to release himself from this dangerous position Ynyr considered himself to be doomed, but in some unknown manner he found himself free, and in thanksgiving founded a church. The place has since been known as Llanvihangel Ystern Llewern, or the Burning Will o' the Wisp.

This journey in the night was probably taken during the battle against the Saxons when, under Ynyr's command, the men of Gwent defeated the Saxons at Llantilio Crossenny. That is what it is called today, but the origination of the name is Llandeilo Croes Ynyr. The native kings of Gwent had a great religious feeling behind their battles with the Saxons, and their victories were invariably celebrated by the founding of a church, just as the final resting place of Tewdrick (Chapter I) was the site of a church founded after the victory at Tintern against the Saxons. The first part of the name indicates the church of Teilo, Bishop of Llandaff and later St Teilo, for it was to him (or rather to the See of Llandaff for ever) that the church was given by Ynyr, or in his memory by his son, Iddon. The second part of the name is simply the cross of Ynyr. A nearby field, I believe, is known as Maes y groes, possibly as this was where the cross was set while the battle was raging.

Llantilio Crossenny is a lovely village. The church stands somewhat above and apart from the few houses in the hollow by the stream. These green lanes are alive with birds, and an orange and white butterfly is likely to rest on one of the many flowers in the high hedgerows. It was here that I met a water diviner from the north country on a scheme for divining water at various farms in Monmouthshire. In these days of the tendency towards settled security, it was unusual to find the diviner saying that he would probably be off with his family to a completely different part of the country when his contract was terminated. He delighted in the country, any part of it, and a new job was all part of his life as long as it has its roots in the soil.

It is a pity that the Hostrey is showing such signs of old age. The old age of buildings should be mellow and dignified, not decrepit, and soon the Hostrey will need too much repair to make it worth while. The old sign shows the arms of Sir David Gilbert, 1415, and also bears the dates 1457–1859, and the date 1900.*

Although founded in the middle of the sixth century, the earliest existing work in the church is twelfth-century, while the later fourteenth and the fifteenth centuries predominate. There are three flat stone monuments of the seventeenth century, two of them bearing the figures of a gentleman and his wife, presumably, on each. The churches of northern Gwent have some very good examples of this type of monument, which I have not found in the churches farther south.

A famous inhabitant of Llantilio was David Gam, whose children were so numerous that they were said to be able to stretch from the church to the door of their house when they stood hand in hand. The house is no longer standing: it was known as Oldcourt, literally translated into

* This old place has now been bought by a brewery company, so perhaps there is hope for it.

Hencwrt, and also known as Henllys, which means, very similarly, the old mansion.

David Gam was an uncertain character in the turbulent days of Glyndwr. He opposed Glyndwr at all times, but once added treachery to his opposition. He suggested he should join Glyndwr's forces, and met the Welsh leader to discuss the situation. His welcome changed to attack, and he attempted to stab Glyndwr as he went towards him. Apart from this, his opposition was normal and active, and he was supported by the Vaughans of Tretower (Roger Vaughan having married one of his daughters, Gwladys) and William ap Thomas of Raglan, who later married Gwladys in her widowhood.

His name was properly David ap Llewellyn, but in the manner of his time a certain disability was converted into a surname. His eye was faulty of vision, possibly there being a turn in it, and this was known as a "gam". There was a taunting verse which Glyndwr was once purported to have recited impromptu to a kinsman of Gam's, beginning, "O' weli di wr coch cam", which translates into something like "If thou see a red-haired squinting man", and goes on to say that Gam's house would be burnt.

When the call came from Henry V for soldiers to fight in France, David Gam answered, and lost his life in loyal service, with other bowmen of Gwent. Both Gam and Roger Vaughan, his son-in-law, were knighted as they lay dying at Agincourt.

It is often said that David Gam was the model for Shakespeare's Fluellen, partly because of his insistence on the King's Welsh birth and his connections with Monmouth, and partly because Llewellyn (David ap Llewellyn) is easily pronounced "Fluellen" by an unaccustomed English tongue. It is also noticeable that the King favours the "care and valour in this Welshman", and the knight-hood at Agincourt points to a similarity again. Yet, in listing the English dead, Davy Gam, esquire, is named, in the presence of Fluellen.

Another "Llantilio" is Llantilio Pertholey, just outside Abergavenny on the Hereford road. The church of St Teilo is of various periods, with its low arches and antiquity of design. There is some beautiful woodwork in this church, which makes it unique in a district of little-known churches with real treasures within them. The pillars of the chapels are of wood, unusual in the county, and the decorated arches are intricately carved, those of the Triley Chapel being Tudor in design: the ceiling is in squared panels, and the wooden divisions are of the same pale wood as the pillars and arches.

On the outside wall of the south aisle are two stone tablets, one saying:

This Wall was made and the Church Repair'd in ye year 1709. Mr Evan James and Mr William Iones being Churchward:

and the other:

This Churchyard was drain'd 1726
Mr Geo. Powell and Mr Wm. Iones of Crossonen
. . . wardens.

The Wernddu Chapel in the church is named for the family who lived at Wernddu, one of the oldest houses in the county, and the original home of the Herberts. The parent line of the family, though not the most distinguished compared, for instance, with the Raglan line or the family at Llanarth, lived there from the twelfth century to the nineteenth century. The family at Wernddu took the name Proger (ap Roger).

Wernddu would appear to derive from "black alders", but, in fact, comes from Gwarin ddu, or Warren the Black, whose daughter, Christian, married Adam ap Herbert, lord of Llanllowell.

Another brother of Gwarin ddu was Gwarin goch, or Warren the Red, whose dwelling became known as Wern gochen. I know these names were given as distinguishing marks in the absence of surnames, but how colourful it all sounds now. (With the recurrence of Welsh surnames, though, no wonder we have to say "Davies the Butcher", and "Davies the Grocer", when they are within a stone's throw of each other: so there is not really so much differ-ence, after all, between the "Warren the Red" of the past and the occupational additions of today.)

This fertile country, while carrying on farming in excellent style, retains its antiquity, without self-con-sciousness, to a remarkable degree. Many of the farms appear to be Tudor or Elizabethan, and almost untouched as far as the exteriors are concerned. All the way around Campston Hill and Graig Serrerthin these farms grow from the land: each one must have its own long history.

I imagine Campston Hill is not used to a great extent, unless one is making for Grosmont without using the main Hereford road. That is a pity, because the views are wide and wonderful. It is similar to the plains and moun-tains seen from the Trellech road, yet the surroundings themselves are, if anything, even more peaceful and beautiful. The lanes are leafy and the fields fertile. On Campston Hill, and all around this district, are numerous examples of early domestic architecture, large and small. One house has an outbuilding with rows of triangular cuts for pigeons to enter.

Llanvihangel Court was rebuilt in the sixteenth century,

and retains the dignity of its period. The whole of Llanvihangel Crucorney, beneath the dark mass of the Skirrid, has a solid, stony appearance. Most of the houses have pointed roofs of an unusual pattern, and the entire village looks of one piece, without the haphazard, variously styled cottages normally making up a village. The ancient stone Skirrid Inn looks as forbidding as the Skirrid Mountain itself. Not for nothing was Llanvihangel Crug Cornel (corner of the rocks) so named.

I went into the church here one summer's day, and a swallow flew round and round, crying its sad cry. I could not see a nest, but there must have been one, because the door was open, and the swallow could have escaped easily had it wished. Yet it seemed frightened, but that must have been because I disturbed its peaceful sanctuary.

In the porch is a verse to James Hughes, who died in 1766:

> My Sledge and Hammer lies reclin'd
> My Bellows too have lost his Wind
> My Fire's extinct my Forge Decay'd
> And in ye Dust my Vice is laid
> My Coal is Spent my Iron is gone
> My nails are Drove my Work is Done.

Near the door is a carved stone of uncertain date, but not later than the first years of the eighteenth century. There is a similar stone, in slightly better condition, at Grosmont, and the ones I have already described at Llantilio Crossenny are of like design. There is good detail of dress, and they have a certain homeliness missing from the more formal effigies. The bodies face forward, but the legs and feet are shown in profile, most noticeable when the subjects are kneeling. These stones add, with their simplicity, to the village church heritage.

Two of the best I know are at Llanvetherine. They are about life-size, one of the Reverend David Powell, rector of the parish for forty-three years, and the other of his wife. They are in excellent condition, especially when it is known that the rector died in 1621. Their clothes give a lovely picture of how a lady and gentleman of that period were clad. Mistress Powell has on her head a tall hat, which must be a Welsh hat.

The top of the Llanvetherine tower overlaps the lower portion. The names comes from Gwytherine, who founded the church in the sixth century, and in the porch is a very ancient stone slab roughly carved with the figure of a priest, with his one arm upraised in blessing, and across the stone is indistinct writing, beginning, "Sant . . .", but this is supposed to have been written only on the surmise, at a later date, that the stone represented St Gwytherine himself.

But among the numerous stones within the church, it is in that of the Reverend David Powell and his delightful wife that Llanvetherine holds its charm for me.

All along the Trothy are old houses, or houses which have foundations of great age. There is Elizabethan Dingestow, and Treowen, one of the earliest Herbert homes, which gave the title to Lord Treowen in comparatively recent days. Wonastow and Troy House, one each side of the river, were two Herbert homes. It was the usual occurrence for an illegitimate son to carry the name of his father, and Sir William Herbert of Troy was such a son of the first Earl of Pembroke. Besides Christian, the daughter of Gwarin ddu, and the mother of the first of the Herbert line, another Christian, some generations later, married George Milborne, and they lived in the old Wonastow Court, where it stands, with its warmly coloured church, above the sloping fields. In a stiff spring breeze I have seen these fields in an endless wave of the bright young green of growing crops. The lodge on that pretty road beneath King's Wood bears the Milborne arms.

The Honddu River lies deep in the valley between ridges which form part of the Black Mountains, and in good weather, at any rate, it combines the serenity of the lowlands with the inevitable aloofness of the mountains. There are trout in the river, which is one of those fairly swiftly moving streams running over flat stones, where it is difficult to see the lazy trout beneath the dappled surface. It is a river where endless time can be spent looking at its changing lights from the little stone bridges along the road. This is the majestic Vale of Ewyas.

It is no rare sight to see a heron standing motionless on a stone in the river.

Writers in the past have commented upon the inaccessibility of the Vale of Ewyas, including the indefatigable Coxe: "I would not recommend timid persons to pass this way in a carriage, for in the whole course of my travels I seldom met with one more inconvenient and unsafe." That was in the early nineteenth century, and other writers have met with similar conditions. The words of the past must have lingered on, for although the roads are now quite good to Llanthony and beyond, and a 'bus jolts its way through the valley several times a day, not many people take advantage of the beauty of the Vale of Ewyas. I have been surprised, at holiday times, when almost every other 'bus in the county has been "standing room only", to find an almost empty vehicle going to Llanthony. I am not complaining for myself, because the quietness of the whole of northern Gwent I find very pleasant, but people do not know what they are missing.

Cwmyoy
Road to Llanthony

Above Fforest is Coalpit Hill, but do not let this deceive you. There was no colliery here, but the name relates to the charcoal-burning that took place in the district.

Near here is Pont Escob, the Bishop's Bridge, for it was here that Bishop Baldwin of Canterbury paused during his great preaching tour in 1188. The whole itinerary was set down by Giraldus Cambrensis who accompanied the Bishop on his tour.

On one side of the Hatteral ridge is Cwmyoy, on the mountainside made jagged by a landslide, its church perched on the slope. Over the hill is Oldcastle, once home of the Lollard, Sir John Oldcastle.

The site of Llanthony Priory was made holy before the tall arches found their perfect setting in the hills. St David himself made holy ground of the solitude of the Black Mountains at Llanthony. So many Welsh names tell a little story within their spelling: Llandewi Nant Honddu, which has become Llanthony, means Church of St David by the Honddu Brook. Michael Drayton's *Polyolbion* of 1622 (the road to Llanthony must have been even worse then than in Coxe's day) tells of the mountainous setting of Llanthony, and throws a light on the ancient Welsh custom of wearing a leek on St David's Day:

'Mongst Hatterill's lofty hills, that with the clouds are
    crown'd,
The Valley Ewias lies, immur'd so deep and round,
As they below that see the mountains rise so high,
Might think the straggling herds were grazing in the sky:
Which in it such a shape of solitude doth bear,
As Nature at the first appointed it for pray'r:
Where in an aged Cell, with moss and ivy grown,
In which not to this day the sun hath ever shone,

Llanthony Abbey
Near Capel-y-ffin

That reverend British Saint, in zealous ages past,
To contemplation liv'd; and did so truly fast,
As he did only drink what crystal Hodney yields,
And fed upon the Leeks he gather'd in the fields.
In memory of whom, in the revolving year,
The Welch-men on his day that sacred herb do wear.
Where, of that holy man, as humbly they do crave,
That in their just defence they might his furtherance have.

Alongside the little church which St David had set up
in the sixth century, a knight, in the late eleventh century
or early twelfth century, having renounced the world,
founded the Priory which was to become the glorious
building which we see in ruins today. William de Lacy, a
Norman knight, came across the seclusion of St David's
Church, and gave up his warrior's ways to seek God. He
completed the repairs to the church by about 1108, and
later his kinsman, Hugh de Lacy, lord of Ewyas, endowed the building of the Priory and William chose to
represent the Augustinian Order.

The Norman church, on its earlier foundations, is very
simple. About one hundred and fifty years ago, sometimes
a little less, sometimes a little more, there must have been
a fashion for a certain style of memorial within the church.
They are mostly blue or grey, with angels' wings in gold:
and what a lot of angels there are on the stones, almost all
of them blowing heartily on trumpets. The verses are full
of warning, but the angels go on blowing. One stone,
dated 1831, sets the tone for the rest:

> Young Men and Maids as you pass by
> As you are now so once was I
> As I am now so Must you be
> Therefore prepare to follow me.

There is such a similarity in the verses that either they were taken from a book of suitable epitaphs or a local poet was commissioned to pay his lasting respects to the deceased.

The bucolic angel faces and numerous verses are not in keeping with their bare Norman surroundings, or with the solitude of the barrier of the surrounding mountains, yet they are quite in keeping with the trend in rural tombstones of the early nineteenth century. Nevertheless, they are in a class of their own. I have seen a similar stone somewhere else, I believe at Llanvetherine.

Beyond the little church and the rising arches of Llanthony Priory, the quiet road goes on through the mountains, or the footpath in the fields follows the course of the road and the river. A snake will sun itself on the road in the first warmth of spring, the first honeysuckle twines in the hedges, and all around the clear air is full of the bleating of the lambs.

One of the first from the outside world (after the monks, who set up another Llanthony in Gloucestershire) to try to conquer the apparently unyielding Vale of Ewyas, was the poet Walter Savage Landor, who purchased the estate for £20,000 in 1807. It was not long before he had antagonised his neighbours (though one would have thought there was sufficient room in the Black Mountains to house Landor and his neighbours), and not many years went by before he left the land which had caused him so much unhappiness. I think Landor would have run into trouble anywhere, such was his character, and certainly his letters to his friends and legal advisers amounted to libel when he discussed the character of his Black Mountain neighbours.

Farther up in the hills is Capel-y-Ffin, and although

this is just out of the county it has always been paired with Llanthony. In fact, when Joseph Leycester Lyne took his monks with him to Capel-y-Ffin, their new abode was known as Llanthony Abbey. It is often thought that he took over the old building, but this was not the case. He began a new building at Capel-y-Ffin, about four miles above the old Priory, and became the first Abbot of Llanthony Abbey.

This remarkable man, who was born in 1837 and died in 1908, was an Anglican monk, known better, perhaps, as Father Ignatius. There are stories of visions in the Vale of Ewyas during his occupation, and his very arrival was tinged with mystery, for the horse drawing the cart became worn out and there was no hope of reaching habitation that night. Most of the monks went on foot, but Father Ignatius had to remain with a child known as "The Infant Samuel" and a casket containing the Sacrament. The horse appeared about to die, and Father Ignatius prayed for help. The horse recovered and drew the little party on through the night without any signs of weariness. That was in 1870, when the Vale of Ewyas was a lonely place.

Some have accused Father Ignatius of showmanship, with his great preaching meetings and faith healings, while others believed in him to the point of worship.

After the death of Father Ignatius the Abbey was eventually deserted.

The next to combine religion with the solemn beauty of the Black Mountains was Eric Gill, the sculptor, the man who brought lettering back to a fine art. This was certainly a family affair, for as well as the brothers of the Ditchling Guild, as they were known, Eric Gill's family lived at Llanthony Abbey too. I think his own words from his *Autobiography* are eloquent, particularly on that sore subject of the cold welcome this lovely country is able to give:

"The monastery at Capel-y-ffin, four miles north-west of Llanthony in the valley of Ewyas, was built in the 1860's by the famous Anglican preacher known as Father Ignatius. His idea was to revive the Benedictine monastic life in the Church of England, but owing to a variety of causes, important among which were his frequently prolonged absences on preaching tours to collect money and the eccentric and fantastic version of the Benedictine Rule which he concocted, the project had been a failure, so that when he died in 1908 there were only three of his monks left and they without money or the approval of the Anglican superiors. These three joined the more recently founded and more successful Anglican Benedictine Abbey on Caldy Island, near Tenby, and so the buildings at Capel became part of the property of that community. The Benedictines of Caldy joined the Roman Church in a body in 1913 and that was how we came to know them. When therefore early in 1924 we heard that they had a disused monastery in the Black Mountains and were willing to consider letting us (*i.e.* the Ditchling Guild) have the place as their tenants, I and another brother went to inspect and report. It was a weirdly exciting business. We arrived about midnight in deep snow, having with great difficulty hired a motor car at Aber-gavenny fifteen miles away. It seemed as though God alone could know where we had got to, if anywhere. For miles and miles we had been driving slowly and dangerously up a narrow and very rough mountain

lane and then we arrived at that dark and almost un-
inhabitable place. There were two monks in charge and
we managed to wake them up.

"That night it certainly seemed an impossible pro-
position, but the next morning, I saw the possibilities
—a quadrangle of outwardly miserable but inwardly
excellent Victorian sham Gothic buildings and, adjoining, the much too big and extravagant beginnings of a
large abbey church. This last was a truly impossible
affair, but the quadrangle, though beginning to go to
ruin, was just the thing for a small community, if they
were prepared to live fifteen miles from a town without
any of the things they call modern conveniences—
except water, and of that there was plentitude; for the
sound of rushing mountain streams was on all sides.
And the surroundings would compensate anybody for
anything."

"And the surroundings would compensate anybody for
anything"—but for one reason and another Eric Gill and
his Guild moved on too, just as Walter Savage Landor had
moved on, and the remaining brothers of Father Ignatius'
Order. They all tried to live amid the splendour of the
Black Mountains, in spiritual communion, but they did
not stay. Perhaps they could not find what they were
seeking. St David lived as a hermit, and William de Lacy
shut himself away from the world, and perhaps those two
were content that it should be so.

The village of Capel does not seem to have been outwardly affected to any great degree by its religious visitors.
The tiny church overshadowed by yew trees and the
chapel beyond built by the Baptists in 1762 serve the
needs of the community, and the monastery is now a

Youth Hostel. One particularly touching epitaph beneath the yews is for little Noah Watkins, aged eight, who said he "would not take a hundred pounds in money for Breaking the Sabbath but keep it holy". What pious little things children were made out to be in 1738.

There is a price on the head of each fox in the mountains, for the lambs are valuable, and this is not hunting country. Last spring I saw a fine fox, so recently shot I thought it was alive: it was golden in the sun, and it lay on a stone beneath the churchyard wall, in the centre of the village.

There is not much protection for the lambs on the mountains, and there is the weather to contend with as well as foxes. In August the sheep are rounded up for their annual dip.

This is real sheep country. In April the lambs, so much whiter than any others I have seen, perform all the gay tricks that only lambs can do. But to the sheep farmer of the hills they are not the gay, irresponsible creatures that the townsman sees. The fields are white with lambs: I have never seen so many. The dread winter of 1947 caused untold losses to the farmers, and even now the numbers have not entirely been made up. That kind of blow is not forgotten in a year or two. The cooing of the wood-pigeons or the song of the lark can make a memory of a little wood or an open meadow, but the sound around Llanthony and the whole of the Honddu Valley will always, to me, be the bleating of the lambs, and the deeper bleating of their mothers, as they are gathered together on the lower slopes of the mountains in the spring.

CONCLUSION

I SOMETIMES think a book of this kind should have a sub-title, perhaps, in this case, "Monmouthshire Miscellany". For everything is in miniature: the family histories (not too numerous, I hope!) are incomplete; the walks through the fields do not include the minute pleasures so personal to the individual; the history is partly posterity's surmise, partly contemporary recording —and how those records differ, one from another.

The old families have been brought in because if I were taking a friend around the county I would point out where "so-and-so" lived: and then a mile or so farther on where a brother or son of the same family might have lived. It gives the old buildings a vestige of life, a life fast fading from most of them, and keeps the county within its boundaries.

Now that I have read the book through I see that there is a predominance of undeniably *Welsh* history and of Welsh place-names. I have always known this to be true; yet, as the Monmouthshire man and his neighbours know, these names are, perhaps, the most Welsh part of Gwent. We speak them with English pronunciation in some sort of Welsh accent. Or is that too complicated for the stranger to the Border lands? Simpler to say that we look more Welsh than we sound. In my Moule's map of Monmouthshire (1836), some of the places are spelled English-fashion: thus Henllys becomes Hentlis, for, on the whole, the man of Monmouthshire automatically anglicises what he sees written in Welsh. That is what I mean when I say we look more Welsh than we sound. The prefix "Llan" is usually "lan", yet, for all that, there is a Welsh inflexion in the voice.

I can take myself as a typical Gwent dweller. Although my father was one generation nearer to Wales than I am myself, and Monmouthshire born, he considered himself an Englishman. Frankly, I do not know what I am (with two Forest of Dean grandmothers), and I rather like it that way. I would not like to be so Welsh that England, and all that she stands for, is an alien thing, and neither would I like to think that I missed the Celtic feeling for music and poetry. The best—and the worst, perhaps—of both worlds? Personally, I do not see much point in the argument. Why not let us remain the Border county that we have been for so long? The individual, if he so cares, can learn Welsh, or send his son to Oxford to take the edge off his voice altogether. It is a matter of choice, and I, for one, like to see a happy medium.

The Gwent folk are friendly, and who is to say from whom they inherit that? It probably became a Border county in the past to be friendly. I do not see why they should have been welcoming in the past, but they are certainly welcoming now, friendly and hospitable.

Gwent is a Border county, and that is all there is to it.

What matters much more is the undulating loveliness of the countryside. The rivers speak a language of their own, a busy, quick talk in the industrial valleys, a more leisurely speech where the Usk and Wye flow. When a Valley choir sings in Welsh the music says whether it is a sad song or a gay song. And the blackbird singing where the boundaries meet sounds the same from either side.

Leland's spelling was of the sixteenth century, but in a few lines he described Gwent quite well as he saw it in his

15   225

day, and, apart from the industrial valleys (and the whimsical spelling), much as it is today:

"The soyle of al Venteland is of a darke reddische yerth ful of slaty stones, and other greater of the same color. The countery is also sumwhat montayneus, and welle replenish'd with woodes, also very fertyle of corne, but men there study more to pastures the which be wel inclosed."

ACKNOWLEDGMENTS

My thanks are offered to all the kind people who have given me information, sometimes interesting in itself, sometimes leading on to other things: to all those who have given me help of any kind. Rather than risk the omission of any name, I will single out only the members of the Newport Library staff, who have always found the books I have wanted, for the Library has been my most consistent source of historical information.

To those long-suffering friends who have walked and talked with me, there is special thanks which can only be given personally.

Acknowledgments and thanks go to the undermentioned publishers and authors for permission to reprint extracts from their works:

Messrs R. H. Johns, Ltd, Newport, for references to various publications; Mr John K. Kennedy and the *Poetry Review* for an extract from "Coaling"; Mr W. J. T. Collins for his Rugby knowledge in Chapter II; Mrs W. H. Davies and Messrs Jonathan Cape, Ltd, for "Days That Have Been" by the late W. H. Davies from his *Collected Poems*; to Mr Idris Davies for "The Curlews of Blaen Rhymni", and with Messrs Faber and Faber, Ltd, for an extract from "The Angry Summer"; to Miss Brenda Watts for part of her late father's poem, "Shall I Forget?"; to Sir H. Idris Bell and the Honourable Society of Cymmrodorion for the translation of Dafydd ap Gwilym's "The Poet makes a house in the birch wood";

to Miss Myfanwy Haycock and the *Western Mail,*
Cardiff, for extracts from "Return" and "July"; to
Mr Raglan Somerset, K.C., and the Fortune Press for
"In Memoriam" from *Twilight and Other Poems*; to
Mrs Eric Gill and Messrs Jonathan Cape, Ltd, for
an extract from the late Eric Gill's *Autobiography*; to
the anthology *Monmouthshire Poetry* (R. H. Johns,
Ltd), compiled by Lawrence Hockey, for the intro-
duction and the renewing of acquaintance with various
poets and poems; and to the Educational Publishing
Company, Cardiff, for an extract from *Songs of Siluria*
by William Williams.

BIBLIOGRAPHY

Borrow, George. *Wild Wales*. 1854.

Bradney, Sir Joseph. *A History of Monmouthshire* (4 vols.). 1907–33.

Cambrensis, Sylvester Giraldus. *The Itinerary of Archbishop Baldwin through Wales*, 1188. 1585.

Cambrian Archæological Association Papers.

Churchyard, Thomas. *The Worthiness of Wales*. 1587.

Clark, J. H. (Usk). *A History of Monmouthshire*. 1869.

—— *Flora of Monmouthshire*.

Collins, W. J. T. *Monmouthshire Writers* (2 vols.). 1945.

—— and Others. *History of the Newport Athletic Club*, 1875–1925.

Coxe, Rev. William. *Historical Tour through Monmouthshire*. 1801.

Davies, Rev. Edward. *Chepstow, a Poem*. 1811.

Davies, Rev. E. T. *A History of the Parish of Mathern*. 1950.

Davies, J. D. Griffith. *Owen Glyn Dŵr*. 1934.

—— *Henry V*. 1935.

Davies, Sir Leonard Twiston. *Men of Monmouthshire* (2 vols.). 1933.

Davies, W. H. *Collected Poems*.

—— *Poet's Pilgrimage*. 1918.

Donovan, E., f.l.s. *Excursions through South Wales and Monmouthshire*. 1805.

Drayton, Michael. *Polyolbion*. 1622.

Eastwood, Dorothea. *A River Diary*. 1950.

Fletcher, John Kyrle. *My Lord Worcester*. 1901.

Gilpin, William. *Observations on the Wye*. 1770.

Hando, Fred J. *The Pleasant Land of Gwent*. 1944.

Havard, Rev. E. *Our Parish* (*the Story of Portskewett with Sudbrooke and St Pierre*). 1948.

Hockey, Lawrence W. (anthology compiled by). *Monmouthshire Poetry*. 1950.

Jones, Rev. Edmund. *A Geographical, Historical and Religious Account of the Parish of Aberystruth in the County of Monmouth*. 1779.

Jones, Thomas, c.h. *Rhymney Memories*. 1938.

Jubilee Book of the Newport High School for Girls, 1896–1946.

Itinerary in Wales of John Leland, 1536–39.

LLOYD, SIR JOHN EDWARD. *A History of Wales (from Earliest Times to Edwardian Conquest)*. 1948.

LOCKE, A. AUDREY. *The Family of Hanbury*. 1916.

MACHEN, ARTHUR. *Far Off Things*.

MALORY, SIR THOMAS. *Morte d'Arthur*.

Monmouthshire and Caerleon Antiquarian Association Papers.

PHILLIPS, ELIZABETH. *A History of the Pioneers of the Welsh Coalfields*. 1925.

PICKFORD, J. A. F. *Between Mountain and Marsh*. 1946.

POWELL, EVAN. *History of Tredegar*. 1884.

ROGERS, NATHAN. *Memoirs of Monmouth-Shire*. 1708.

SOTHEBY, W. *A Tour through Parts of Wales*. 1794.

TENNYSON, LORD ALFRED. *Idylls of the King*.

The Wit and Wisdom of Lord Tredegar. 1911.

The Triads.

WATERS, IVOR (compiled by). *A Chepstow and Tintern Anthology*. 1948.

—— *Inns and Taverns of the Chepstow District*. 1948.

WILLIAMS, A. H. *An Introduction to the History of Wales*. 1948.

WILLIAMS, CHARLES HENRY. *Legends of Gwent*. 1857.

WILLIAMS, DAVID. *History of Monmouthshire*. 1796.

INDEX

Cardiff, 10, 18, 40, 52, 62, 67: Rugby
Team, 54
Carnivals, 64–6
Carp, 201
Cashmore's Yard, 47
Castell Arnallt, 157–8
Castell Meredydd, 12, 69
Castell y Bwch, 102
Castleton, 18: Beagles, 21
Cas Troggy, 139, 163, 167–8: Brook,
162, 167–8
Catchmay (family of), 189
Catchmead, Tracy, 173
Cattle Market, Newport, 9
Cecils (Llanover family of), 148
Cefngoleu, 83
Cefn-Ila, 130
Cefn Mabli, 67, 69: Arms, 68, 97
Cefn Tilla Court, 138, 142
Cefn-vynach, 100
Celts, 2, 127, 225
Chapel Farm Llandevaud, 132
Chapels (general), 16, 61, 63, 66, 91
Charcoal, 151, 217
Charles I, 13, 25, 26, 130, 142, 172,
174, 182
Charles II, 35, 142, 165, 174
Charter of the Forests, 170–5
Chartists, 43–6, 175
Chepstow, 1, 7, 8, 25, 37, 130, 133,
142, 157, 161, 162, 171, 180–4, 185,
186, 190, 191, 197: Castle, 174, 180,
182–3: Church, 182, 183–4: lords
of, 167, 182, 193: lordship of, 141:
Racecourse, 191
Chepstow Park Wood, 133, 162, 185,
186
Chestnuts, 31
Chief Commissioner of Works, 148
Cholera, 82
Christchurch, 7, 24, 122, 127, 177–8
Church House Inn, Newport, 54
Church House Inn, St Bride's, 16
Churches (general), 9, 16, 169–70
Churchyard, Thomas, 86, 121–2, 135,
140–1, 200
Cistercians, 99, 124, 193, 208

Civil War, 13, 25, 35, 39, 40, 130,
139–40, 142, 172, 182
Clayton, Richard, 184
Cluniacs, 56
Clytha Castle, 145–6: Church, 152,
202: House, 145, 147: lords of, 152,
202
Coal, 8, 59–118 mentioned, 121, 151
Coalpit Hill, 217
Coastal area, 8, 10–37
Coed Bedw, 69
Coed Cefn Pwll-du, 67, 69
Coed Craig Ruperra, 69
Coedkernew, 10
Coed-y-Defaid, 88
Coed-y-ffern, 186
Coity Mountains, 113
Coldbrook, 42, 109, 124, 156–7, 159
Coll, 163
Collins, W. J. T. ("Dromio"), 51,
53
Common Coed, 22
Common Coed-y-Paen, 129
Corn Laws, 44
Coronation Scot, 115
Coulman, E., 51
Covent Garden, 80
Coward, Noel, 113
Cowslips, 29
Coxe, Rev. William, 26, 38, 75, 115,
136, 141, 152, 161, 216, 217
Cradock (Llangwm family of), 134:
Walter, 134, 169
Craig-y-Dorth, 189
Crawshay, Alfred, 136: Richard, 75,
91, 95
Crick, 25, 171, 173
Cricket, 50, 93, 135
Crindau House, 41
Crimea War, 15, 104
Croes-y-mwyalch, 99
Cromwell, Oliver, 25, 35, 41, 133, 143,
182, 183
Cross Keys, 75
Crouchback, Edmund, 202, 204
Crows, 74
Crucifixion, 80, 145, 157